PHONETICS

A critical analysis of phonetic
theory and a technic for the practical
description of sounds

PHONETICS

A critical analysis of phonetic
theory and a technic for the practical
description of sounds

by
Kenneth L. Pike

Ann Arbor: The University of Michigan Press

FOREWORD

THIS volume by Kenneth Lee Pike has grown out of some seven years of practical experience in the field attempting to analyze and describe the sounds of a number of non-Indo-European languages. For much of this time Dr. Pike lived among the Mixtecos in southwestern Mexico, an Indian people numbering about 200,000. The language of these people he has mastered and is describing in several monographs. His experience, however, has not been limited to this particular language. As the phonetics specialist of the Wycliffe Bible Translators who have language investigators working in each of the important Indian languages of Mexico, and as the professor of phonetics of the Summer Institute of Linguistics in which these and other such investigators are trained, he has assisted in analyzing and describing the sounds of a wide variety of the languages of so-called primitive peoples. *Phonetics*, which is now followed by a second [1] and a third volume on related subjects, first reviews critically the basic assumptions of phonetic theory and then proceeds to clarify and restate many of these assumptions. Upon this foundation the author constructs basic definitions and classifications of such items as phone, syllable, stop, vowel, and consonant, and provides a descriptive order in which all sounds may be described in relation to their productive mechanisms.

The end sought is the description of any sound apart from speech in order that factors of speech may not give undue influence to the terminology applied to it. To accomplish this end it was necessary to examine the relationship between speech and nonspeech sounds and to establish a technic of description which could deal with *all* nonsense sounds and syllables as well as with those of language. In other words, it was necessary to divorce pure phonetics, the description of the nature and formation of sounds, from phonemics, the function of sounds in speech. This volume, therefore, does not deal with the speech function of sounds, nor with the practical methods for finding the phonemes of a language, nor even with the formation of phonetic

---

[1] The second volume, *Tone Languages* (University of Michigan Press), deals with the nature of tonal systems and provides a technic for the analysis of their significant pitch contrasts.

v

orthographies. In fact, it is not a conventional " practical phonetics " book.

The present volume is not " impractical," however, because it covers only one part of the field. On the contrary, the material here presented is eminently practical in that it provides the data which places speech in a new perspective. It leads the investigator to see that sounds have a subphonemic segmentation which underlies all speech and actually limits the forms into which languages are approximately molded. In addition, it lays the groundwork for a different approach to phonemic units by way of segmental units — an approach which is already proving of value in experimental classes given to research workers in the phonemic field.

This reworking of phonetic theory should prove of great value in another direction. It seems now to be fairly well recognized that an instrumental study of the acoustic reality of sounds or of the physical minutiae of their production has little practical bearing upon language problems until it has been correlated with the perceptual reactions of speakers to these sounds. These perceptual reactions must be classified *in some way*. Often those who deny the necessity of any perceptual correlations really use perceptual classifications of an extremely naïve type. It is to be hoped that laboratory technicians will find the new classifications offered here of considerable assistance in providing the perceptual assumptions basic to the interpretation of the actual physical data which they uncover.

The chief practical contribution of this volume, however, may be to those students of general phonetics who intend to reduce to writing the languages which are as yet without literature. To these students this contribution will not be the furnishing of specific technics for alphabet formation,[2] but the provision of the technical background for the analysis of sounds which is prerequisite to any such technics. Specific alphabet-forming technics are of little value to an investigator who cannot recognize and transcribe sounds — and features of sounds are most readily recognized when the total system of sound production is understood. The present volume provides this basic analysis of the formation of sounds.

Charles C. Fries

---

[2] The third volume, *Phonemics* (University of Michigan Press), provides for this correlative need.

CONTENTS

ILLUSTRATIONS

PRODUCTIVE MECHANISMS

CONTROLLING MECHANISMS

PART I

PHONETIC THEORY: A CRITICAL ANALYSIS

INTRODUCTION

PRESENT phonetic classifications are based on a limited number of sounds. Many sounds actually occurring in speech, in addition to many types which have not been found in language, are frequently ignored, while others are mentioned but briefly or, if discussed at all, grouped together into small unorganized sections where they fail to contribute their potential share to the establishment of adequate analyses. Different kinds of data have contributed to the analysis and classification of vocal sounds. Movements of the vocal organs have given the basis for physiological description, but this material has been modified by the acoustic nature of the sounds and by the function which they perform in speech systems. Many fundamental assumptions which have never been adequately stated have become established in phonetic descriptions. These assumptions have tended to conceal the relationship between the various types of data, and a number of them have discouraged the investigation of certain sounds that would have called attention to many of the assumptions themselves.

Part I of the study here presented reviews phonetic theory in several of its fundamental phases in an attempt to weigh the factors involved in some of these problems. Chapter I shows the minor place given in phonetic literature to many types of sound that occur in speech, and discusses some of the reasons for the difference in treatment between these sounds and those which are accorded more prominence. The second half of the chapter describes briefly four possible methods for investigating sounds and indicates which one has been employed for the analysis of the material underlying this study, with certain reasons for its choice. Chapter II points out additional sound types which current phonetic classifications tend to ignore and calls attention to other undefined assumptions underlying this neglect, but here the sounds discussed are one step further removed from speech. The boundary line between the sounds considered in the first chapter as contrasted with those discussed in the second is somewhat vague, chosen perhaps as much for convenience as on the basis of structure.

3

Chapter III shows some of the problems involved in cutting a continuous stream of speech into segments. It postulates the existence
of a nonfictitious phonetic segmentation which is not dependent upon
phonemic divisions, but which to a large extent conditions those divisions; the segment itself is not defined until Chapter VII. Chapter
IV brings forward evidence that the cavities of the vocal mechanism do
not have identical functions in producing sound, and that closures, or
partial strictures, or movements likewise have varied places in the
economy of sound production. Many of these differences are shown
to comprise basic and essential assumptions in all articulatory descriptions of sounds which must be retained but which should be defined.
Chapter V traces the mixture of articulatory, acoustic, and phonemic
criteria in consonant–vowel differentiation. It suggests the elimination of certain of the criteria and the expansion of others. Part I
analyzes various key difficulties in phonetic description. After these
factors have been reviewed, Part II presents a constructive system
which attempts to embody the suggestions contained in this analysis.

CHAPTER I

MARGINAL SOUNDS

SOUNDS occurring infrequently as phonemic norms, or appearing but rarely in certain set types of speech, comprise a group of *marginal* speech sounds. Data which they can contribute to a phonetic analysis tend to be neglected or given too little weight in the establishment of basic phonetic classifications. The explanation for the shunting of marginal sounds to one side seems to be the assumption of standards of normality for the selection of those speech sounds which are allowed to contribute criteria for the establishment of basic classes.

Many investigators [1] in defining vowels include as one of the essential characteristics that all vowels should be voiced, rejecting other varieties as abnormal. Jones, for example, says that " whispered speech is not regarded as normal." [2] Westermann and Ward use almost identically the same words.[3] Noël-Armfield, as if it were not sufficient to exclude whisper from vowel definition,[4] discusses it in a small section [5] together with inverse sounds, clicks, and consonants with glottal closure — types entirely extraneous. Passy does likewise, both in excluding it from his definition of vowel,[6] and in relegating it to a small section [7] containing rather rare speech sounds

---

[1] Gairdner, *The Phonetics of Arabic*, 11; Jones, *An Outline of English Phonetics* [4], § 97, see also § 255 and p. 23 n.; Kenyon, *American Pronunciation* [6], 57–58; Nicholson, *A Practical Introduction to French Phonetics*, 9; Noël-Armfield, *General Phonetics* [4], 8, 31; Passy, *Petite phonétique comparée* [3], 14; *idem*, *The Sounds of the French Language* [2], 56; Ripman, *Elements of Phonetics*, 10; Stirling, *The Pronunciation of Spanish*, 6; Sweet, *A Primer of Phonetics* [3], 13; Viëtor, *German Pronunciation* [5], 7; see also Fletcher, *Speech and Hearing*, 5, 7. For further discussion of vowel definition see Chapter V.

[2] Jones, 23 n.

[3] Westermann and Ward, *Practical Phonetics for Students of African Languages*, 13.

[4] Noël-Armfield, 8 n.

[5] Noël-Armfield, 120–23.

[6] Passy, *Sounds*, 56; *Phonétique*, 14.

[7] Passy, *Sounds*, 86–88; *Phonétique*, 110–13.

(clicks [8]), rare variants of speech sounds (inverse [9]), and nonspeech sounds (whistle [10]). These, and elsewhere glides [11] also, he calls " accessories," [12] giving ample evidence that he considers them abnormal. Even more surprising as " accessories of language " are expression of the face, gesture, and the language of signs.[13] This classification is made in spite of the fact that he lists whisper as occurring regularly in some languages.[14]

Although whisper is thus given an unsatisfactory classification, it is discussed or at least mentioned in many places.[15] Related problems of breathed or voiceless vowels,[16] and " voiced [h]," [17] receive less attention.

Conditions of the vocal cords other than those associated with voice, whisper, and breath are usually completely ignored. Singing is used for an occasional illustration.[18] Vibrato is not considered.[19] Falsetto is rarely mentioned.[20] Types of vocal trill or murmur are not clearly differentiated, but a few receive passing notice.[21]

The second major criterion of normal usage often applied is that

[8] Passy, *Sounds*, 86–87; *Phonétique*, 113.
[9] Passy, *Sounds*, 110–12; *Phonétique*, 86.
[10] Passy, *Sounds*, 88; *Phonétique*, 113.
[11] Passy, *Sounds*, 89.
[12] Passy, *Sounds*, 86; *Phonétique*, 110.
[13] Passy, *Sounds*, 89.
[14] *Ibid.*, 87.
[15] Bloomfield, *Language*, 95, 102; Curry, *The Mechanism of the Human Voice*, 30–31; Gairdner, 11, 32; Jones, 23 n., §§ 82, 89; Kenyon, 38, 49; *idem* in *Webster's New International Dictionary of the English Language* [2], §§ 16, 44 (10); Noël-Armfield, 8 n., 121–22; Passy, *Sounds*, 15, 56, 87; Ripman, 7, 21; Sweet, 10, 12, 22–23, 28; Westermann and Ward, 13, 85.
See also C. B. Miller, *An Experimental-phonetic Investigation of Whispered Conversation;* D. C. Miller, *The Science of Musical Sounds*, 235; Rousselot, *Principes de phonétique expérimentale* (New Ed.), 468–78.
[16] Jespersen, *The Articulations of Speech Sounds Represented by Means of Analphabetic Symbols*, 70–71; Kenyon, 47, 139; *idem* in Webster, § 44 (10); Noël-Armfield, 31, n. 1; Sweet, 22.
[17] Jones, § 779; Kenyon, 47; *idem* in Webster, § 44 (10); Noël-Armfield, 30; Ripman, 21.
[18] Jones, 70 n.; Passy, *Sounds*, 55; Ripman, 13; Sweet, 53–54, 66–69.
[19] But see *The Vibrato*, edited by Seashore (*Univ. Iowa Studies, Studies in the Psychology of Music*, Vol. I).
[20] Curry, 46–47; Sweet, 10; Rousselot, 252 (and 479–82 for ventriloquism); Duyff " Petite contribution à la connaissance de la voix de fausset," *Arch. Néer. Phon. Expér.*, 4 (1929), 67–71 [with bibliography].
[21] Bloomfield, 95, 99, 101, 102, 112; Jespersen, 32, 75.

a sound should be made with air leaving the lungs. Passy says, " All speech sounds have their origin in a single physiological act — respiration — modified in various ways." [22] Later in the same work [23] he distinguishes between clicks, which have no air going below the glottis, and inverse sounds. The contradiction is explainable only on the ground that in the first instance Passy included sounds which he considered normal, and hence that clicks are not normal and therefore excluded. The abnormality of clicks in his opinion is further evidenced by their being given but slight space in an unclassified catch-all section of " accessory sounds." [24]

Ripman states that a current of air from the lungs " is the essential element of all speech," [25] without discussing click types; he does mention " inhaled [inverse] breath." [26]

Kenyon makes no qualification of his statement, " The sounds of speech are produced by breath forced from the lungs and modified by the vocal organs," [27] except by implication when he says of stops, " Outward breath-pressure is assumed in all cases." [28] The fact that he is dealing with just one language will not completely explain his assumption when other writers [29] show various types of inverse and click sounds as interjections in English.[30] Elsewhere he mentions interjectional sounds not in the English phonemic system [31] and, also, even foreign sounds.[32]

These quotations reflect the normative attitude of other writers, but are more strongly phrased. Noël-Armfield's chapter which discusses clicks and inverse sounds has,[33] like Passy's, no organization except as a container of what he thus implies are abnormalities; in it the presence of whispered sounds which he had previously excluded from his basic phonetic classification [34] suggests that these other

[22] Passy, *Sounds*, 6; " General Discussions of Respiration and Its Modification," 6–9.

[23] Passy, *Sounds*, 87.　　[25] Ripman, 1.　　[27] Kenyon, 38.

[24] See n. 12.　　[26] Ripman, 2. .　　[28] Kenyon, 40.

[29] Bloomfield, 94; Noël-Armfield, 120–21; Sweet, 43.

[30] I personally know a speaker of American English who now and again uses glottalized stops as variants of [t] and implosive stops as variants of [b]. Jones, § 571, mentions ejectives occasionally employed by French people.

[31] Kenyon, 47–48: [m̥m̥m; m̥m?m].

[32] Kenyon, 48: [l̥].

[33] Noël-Armfield, 121–23.

[34] Noël-Armfield, 8 n., 31 n.

sounds are also excluded. As late as 1912 the alphabet of the International Phonetic Association included merely symbols for sounds made by air from the lungs only.[35]

Various writers discuss or refer to types of stops made without air from the lungs: glottalized stops (ejectives),[36] implosives (glottalic clicks),[37] clicks (velaric clicks),[38] and egressive clicks (reverse clicks).[39] When sounds made with air entering the lungs receive mention,[40] they are treated perhaps with slightly less feeling of abnormality.

Sounds produced or modified by larynx, pharynx, false vocal cords, and epiglottis are often considered abnormal in spite of the physiological normality of their processes. These sounds are paid but scant attention [41] in description of the vocal apparatus. They seem little understood, since they are difficult to produce and, furthermore, have but slight place in phonemic systems.

Certain sonorants, [l], [r], [m], [n], are considered perfectly

[35] *The Principles of the International Phonetic Association* (Supplement to *Le Maître Phonétique*), 10.

[36] Bell, *Visible Speech* (Inaugural Ed.), 126; Bloomfield, 99; Jones, § 570; Noël-Armfield, 3, 122; Sweet, 59; Westermann and Ward, 96.

[37] Bloomfield, 93–94 (suction sounds); Passy, *Sounds,* 87; Sweet, 43; Ward, *An Introduction to the Ibo Language,* 6; Westermann and Ward, 92.

[38] Bell, 56, 126; Bloomfield, 93–94; Jespersen, *Lehrbuch der Phonetik* [4], 124; Noël-Armfield, 120–21; Passy, *Sounds,* 87; Sweet, 7; Westermann and Ward, 98.

[39] Bell, 62.

[40] Noël-Armfield, 120; Passy, *Sounds,* 86; Ripman, 2; Sweet, 43.

[41] For mention of larynx or pharynx see Curry, 37, 74, 155–56; Jones, 70, n. 15; Muckey, *The Natural Method of Voice Production,* 18, 85, 145; Noël-Armfield, 4–5, 107, 109–12; Passy, *Sounds,* 9; Ward, "Phonetic Phenomena in African Languages," *Archiv für vergleichende Phonetik,* 1 (1937), 51; Westermann and Ward, 85. Compare sounds of " bronchial tubes " mentioned in Passy, *Sounds,* 84; Sweet, 12. See also Carmody, "An X-Ray Study of Pharyngeal Articulation," *Univ. Calif. Publ. Mod. Philol.,* 21, No. 5 (1941), 377–84.

For mention of false vocal cords see Jespersen, *Articulations,* 14; Jones, § 82; Muckey, 70–73; Ripman, 5; Russell, *Speech and Voice,* 232, 236–37; Sweet, 8.

For mention of epiglottis see Doke, " The Phonetics of the Zulu Language " (*Bantu Studies,* Vol. 2, Special Number), 33; Negus, *The Mechanism of the Larynx,* 39–44, 229, 449; Noël-Armfield, 4–5; Passy, *Sounds,* 12; Russell, 210–14; idem, *The Vowel,* 117–26.

For mention of lungs see Russell, *Speech and Voice,* 215–17.

For discussion of the action of the laryngeal ventricle see Pepinsky, " The Laryngeal Ventricle Considered as an Acoustical Filter," *Journ. Acoust. Soc. Am.,* 14 (1942), 32–35.

normal when voiced; the voiceless relationship [42] provides a problem similar to that of the vowels (see " Classification Criteria," Chapter V).

Back unrounded and front rounded vowels are frequently treated as abnormal,[43] in contrast to front unrounded and back rounded vowels.

Many writers,[44] especially those dealing with single languages, make no mention of any of the marginal sounds discussed above except for items from the last group when they are phonemic in the language studied. In general, these writers are the same as those who make no mention of nonspeech sounds.[45] The advantage which such writers, and especially teachers of phonetics of single languages, may gain by the utilization of marginal and nonspeech sounds will be discussed later (p. 24).

Within the description of sounds as a whole, much is to be desired. The assumption that only egressive air from the lungs is normal has shut off many comparative data to be derived from clicks, glottalized stops, and the like, data which would have led to the description of more factors concerning air streams and their chambers and passageways. No discussion shows that both compression and rarefaction (in turn) may be applied to any sound type; no attempt is made, for example, to find vowels with a click mechanism or trills with pressure from the larynx.

The extent of an air chamber seems not to be defined; the difference between the function of the mouth chamber during a nasal consonant and its function in oral vowel production is not fitted into a system of air chambers. The varying usage of closures and partial strictures for limiting such chambers as distinct from causing air pressure or rarefaction by their movement, or causing friction by their impeding of an air stream remains unclassified. See " Structural Function " (pp. 56–65, 129–36) for fuller discussion of the functional

[42] I have found no clear presentation of the problem, but cf. Jones, 24, n. 3; Kenyon, 47–48, 60, 127, 157; Noël-Armfield, 26–27, 82, 108.

[43] Passy, *Sounds*, 58–60; *Phonétique,* 94–95. For secondary cardinal vowels see Jones, 35; Noël-Armfield, 16.

[44] Forchhammer, *How to Learn Danish* [4]; Jones and Woo, *A Cantonese Phonetic Reader;* Karlgren, *A Mandarin Phonetic Reader (Archives d'Études Orientales,* Vol. 13) ; Nicholson; Viëtor.

[45] See p. 34, n. 25.

differences. Presumably failure to perceive the relationship of the glottal stop to its pressure chamber is what caused Jones to say that it is " neither breathed nor voiced "[46] (in contrast to other stops which may be either).

Although in regard to glottalized stops various investigators[47] have mentioned the rising action of the larynx to achieve the compression required, and others, less felicitously, have mentioned in that connection, or in relation to clicks, an " inner closure,"[48] yet I find no evidence of anyone's hunting for a stricture having the same function but lying in reverse position (i.e. outward in respect to the releasing stricture). Such phenomena can be found (see pp. 88, 101–2); they are more important for forcing classification of types of air chambers and functions of strictures, the abandonment of casual assumptions, than for their own frequency of occurrence.

The relegation of nonpulmonic sounds to an obscure place or their entire omission has brought with it the obscuring of basic sound production. No one, especially not a beginning student of phonetics, can expect to grasp the vocal panorama of the possibilities of compression and rarefaction when only one compressive type is given.

The middle ground of percussion (pp. 103–5) apart from compression and rarefaction seems to be relatively unexplored, but serves to emphasize the classification by delineating its border lines and explaining a few puzzling transitional sounds, or the sounds resulting from the opening and closing of the lips while the remainder of the vocal mechanism is motionless (but while a closure is maintained at the glottis or the back part of the tongue; the same effect may be obtained by snapping the outside of the throat or cheek while the glottis is closed). The quiescent air chambers for these sounds must also be classified.

To obscure further the possibility of recognition of a full gamut of stops, fricatives, nasals, and so on produced by each of the various pressure–rarefaction mechanisms, stops are the only types of nonpulmonic mechanisms mentioned in the textbooks; fricatives and nasals find no place whatsoever. Noël-Armfield's chart, " The Main

[46] Jones, § 553.

[47] Jones, § 570; Sweet, 59.

[48] Bell, 62; cf. also 56 (" suction stopper "); Bloomfield, 99; Westermann and Ward, 96.

Types of Human Speech Sounds," [49] demonstrates the point; three clicks are the only nonpulmonic sounds recorded, and these are listed on the chart in the same place as the plosives (i.e. stops).

Certain types of voiced " glottalized continuants " [50] disguise this lack of nonpulmonic fricatives; actually such continuants are produced by air from the lungs, and not at all by the mechanism of rising larynx which produces glottalized stops (but sometimes the two types may be parallel phonemically if not phonetically).

I find no adequate description of the combination, or possibilities of combination, of pulmonic types with nonpulmonic types. Nasalized clicks are well enough known,[51] but if terminology has not been built up which is adequate for describing the chambers and structural functions of the separate types, still less has it been provided for the combinations.

Because present classifications eliminate much marginal material from basic consideration they tend to lead to a feeling of false security, so that students, thinking them complete, may fail to look for more sound types, or may have their perception dulled to the implications of new items which they might discover. This limitation of sound types in classifications has prevented the development of a terminology which would describe many items of sound that almost certainly exist in language, although at present they are unreported. The failure to develop classifications and terminology for nonspeech sounds in an inclusive system with speech sounds and marginal sounds militates in the same direction (see Chapter II for discussion of nonspeech factors).

Normative prejudice causes in part the selection of classification criteria which cannot be strictly applied, and leaves contradictions in the material. The most important instance is that of vowel and consonant differentiation (see Chapter V, " Classification Criteria ").

Present phonetic descriptions are a hybrid, being neither strict description by physiological structure and movement alone (with or without acoustic judgments added), nor statements designed solely to show systems of sound in speech (which should be the province of

[49] Noël-Armfield, chart facing 180.

[50] See Sapir, " Glottalized Continuants in Navaho, Nootka and Kwakiutl (with a Note on Indo-European)," *Lang.*, 14 (1938), 248–74.

[51] See Westermann and Ward, 100.

the phonemicist). The exclusion of whispered and voiceless vowels from vowel definition, the inconsistency of the boundary line between consonants and vowels, the inclusion of certain types of laterals but not others in phonetic charts, the relegation to a minor place of non-pulmonic sounds and of pharyngeal sounds, the exclusion of nonspeech sounds, all point to the fact that judgments of normality are judgments of phonemic usage, not of phonetic character, and as such they are to be deprecated. Not only speech values as a whole are allowed to affect the classification, but even certain very specialized speech values which are chosen as norms.

Why does no language use exclusively whispered vowels? Why, do certain nonspeech sounds never occur in language? Why are some rare and others frequent? Rarity and frequency of occurrence of phonetic sound types as phonemes or variants of phonemes should be investigated by the phonemicist, but the phonetician is doing him no favor when he prejudges the conclusions by giving normalized classifications, and suppresses the very data that would provide the phonemic choice of sounds with a contrastive setting.

Whenever a system of phonetic description is affected by one or more phonemic systems, it automatically and proportionately prevents the unbiased description of a new phonemic system (that is, a new language), or of sounds in isolation apart from a phonemic system, or of sounds of a language before the phonemic system has been detected, or, for that matter, of any material for which a strict phonetic record is desired within the limits of the technic.

The material for this volume was presented to phonetic discussion groups at Ann Arbor [52] in the summers of 1939 and 1940. During the session of 1940 Dr. Bernard Bloch [53] called to my attention the fact that J. C. Catford had independently arrived at certain of these conclusions and published them in an excellent though short article [54] to which I had not had access.

Catford also objects to keeping implosives, ejectives, and clicks

[52] The groups met at the Linguistic Institute (under the auspices of the Linguistic Society of America and the University of Michigan).

[53] Dr. Bloch is associated with the Linguistic Atlas of the United States and Canada.

[54] Catford, "On the Classification of Stop Consonants," *Le Maître Phonétique,* 3d Series, 65 (1939), 2–5.

apart, " as if they don't enter into a general classification along with other consonants," [55] and regards that procedure as pedagogically unsound.

Starting from the description of " pulmonic," " glottalic," and " velaric " clicks given by Beach,[56] he enlarges the classification to cover not only these " suction stops " but also " pressure stops," and does so with an admirably lucid terminology and systematic presentation. He suggests extending the classification to fricatives,[57] and gives an illustration or two.

His description of voiced implosives (glottalic suction stops) [58] is accurate and clear; later he describes voiced (velaric) clicks.[59] Placing the two descriptions together, one finds he has not discussed various possibilities of combination of his three basic types of stops, and has failed completely to try to correlate the two descriptions into a single system of type combinations which would have suggested many other (speech and nonspeech) forms. Such a system should explain, for example, the two simultaneous but different functions of the velar closure during the voiced (velaric) click (the term " inner closure," used also by Bell,[60] obscures this difference), as well as delimit the possible types of sounds of each mechanism which could be superimposed one on the other; in addition, the relationship of the functional parts of the air chambers involved should have been made clear.

Catford's classification is primarily for stops, and, in spite of his reference to fricatives, fails to show another basic point, that each mechanism for making sounds can produce just the same fricative, lateral, nasal, and vocalic types except for certain innate limitations (including, for example, lack of audibility in click vowels and impossibility of glottal stop with the air chamber of a [velaric] click).

[55] *Ibid.*, 2.

[56] Beach, *The Phonetics of the Hottentot Language.* This work I did not see until 1940.

[57] Catford, *op. cit.* in *Le Maître Phonétique,* 3d Series, 65 (1939), 2, 5. Further search has shown that Jones had earlier described fricatives (and stops, trills, and so on) of implosives and click types in " Implosive and Click Sounds," *Le Maître Phonétique,* 3d Series, 22 (1907), 111–14.

[58] Catford, *op. cit.* in *Le Maître Phonétique,* 3d Series, 65 (1939), 4.

[59] *Ibid.*, 4–5.

[60] Bell, 62.

Nor does Catford try to show that the pressure–rarefaction phenomena described in his three types of speech sounds are even more widely applicable, demonstrable as the basis for all nonspeech sounds except those at the halfway mark (see percussives, pp. 103–5) and a further small residue (see p. 105, scrapives).

This study attempts to present a more universal classification of marginal speech and nonspeech sounds than any now available. No effort has been made here to achieve extreme minuteness of detail in regard to point of articulation; but, on the other hand, every sound which seems to demand a modification of present classifications, or which is a new type, has been given place regardless of its apparent lack of importance in communication. Since the line of demarcation between speech and nonspeech types is not sharp (see, however, pp. 149–51), many types actually analyzed are not specifically mentioned when they can be subsumed under the classifications as presented and illustrated.

The *auditory articulation technic* (or, more briefly, the *articulatory technic*) has been employed for analysis; by this are meant description in terms of movements and positions of the vocal organs and investigation primarily by the ear and the kinesthetic sense. When investigation of articulations utilizes instruments, the extended procedure represents the *instrumental articulatory technic*. In contrast to these, *auditory acoustic technic* and *instrumental acoustic technic* analyze and describe the sounds (or sound waves) themselves rather than the movements producing them. The rest of this chapter will be devoted to a consideration of the limitations and advantages of each of these four technics in relation to phonetic classification. The first to be discussed will be the *articulatory technic,* as already defined in this paragraph.

In phonetic literature [61] sounds are occasionally mentioned which, although the same or very similar, are produced by a sharply different action of the vocal mechanism, a difference readily seen by the eye or noted by the kinesthetic sense. The articulatory technic simply describes alternate means for the production of one sound.

[61] See Bloomfield, 108; Jones, *Outline,* 102, n. 6, 200 n.; Kenyon, 156; Ripman, 53; Sweet, 29–30.

A different situation prevails when the articulatory variation is minute. Sweet's statement that each new tongue position produces a new vowel, and hence that the number of vowel sounds is infinite,[62] is only a partial truth. True, there may be a difference in the sound waves which instruments could record, but the ear is not infinitely delicate. For changes of all types the ear (with individual variation around a norm) has definite thresholds of discrimination beyond which it cannot go. This limits possibilities of discrimination between all sound elements, whether differences caused by minute changes of point of articulation or differences of prosodic factors of pitch, quantity, and stress.[63] The articulatory procedure, therefore, does not attempt to describe an infinite variety of sounds and articulatory positions, but only those above the perceptual threshold; the number which can be perceptually discriminated is not infinite.

The thresholds of discrimination are present even when sounds are contrasted one directly following the other. Any phonetician knows from practical experience that this power of discrimination is extraordinarily reduced if the sounds are not given contiguously; that is, if two very similar vowels are pronounced one after the other it may be relatively simple to say that they are different, but to identify which of the two appears in a sentence may be impossible. Persons without phonetic training come far short in their discriminatory powers of that of which the ear is basically capable. Jones states that a good (i.e. expert) ear can distinguish well over fifty vowels (apart from nasalized or retroflex types and the like);[64] this number is considerably short of an infinite variety.

This perceptual factor must be taken into account in any definition of a phonetic unit (see below, pp. 45–46, 108–10) or else no two phoneticians can agree on procedure when at times they perceive dif-

---

[62] Sweet, 13.

[63] See Fletcher, Part III, Chapter II (" Limits of Audition "), 145–66 (" Minimum Perceptible Differences of Sound "), 134 (Bibliography) ; *idem,* " Loudness, Masking and Their Relations to the Hearing Process and the Problem of Noise Measurement," *Journ. Acoust. Soc. Am.,* 9 (1938), 275–93; Shohara, " An Experimental Study of the Control of Pronunciation," *Speech Monographs,* 6 (1939), 105–10. Dr. Shohara measured considerable deviation in pitch and especially in duration even when subjects tried to control their rate of speaking and to keep it steady.

[64] Jones, *Outline,* § 122.

ferent entities. The factor reaches difficult proportions, since the perceptual element is highly variable and is conditioned by phonemic background.[65]

In contrast with the articulatory technic, which allows one to produce unknown sounds from articulatory descriptions (in the manner of a cook book), a supplementary descriptive method, the *imitation-label technic,* merely gives names to known sounds. The latter places labels on standards otherwise established, whereas the former establishes rough standards. The imitation-label technic may employ written " descriptions " of sounds. Here, however, the sound cannot be produced by following the description. Such descriptions are labels only; rather than serving as directions to produce the sound, they are merely convenient tags by which to recall to mind or to mention certain sounds previously learned by imitation following a demonstration. The label itself is unimportant; any will serve, since its accuracy of description is entirely immaterial to its application. Demonstration (from the point of view of the teacher) and imitation (from the point of view of the pupil) are the all-important factors; the label merely serves to recall the transaction. Much language is learned by imitation (by listening to it spoken, or from phonograph records and the like), without labels being applied to the sounds. When labels are applied to sounds learned from imitation, with or without a feeling that the labels are articulatory descriptions, the imitation-label technic has been used.

Sometimes extraordinary difficulty is encountered in determining which technic one is employing, since one can so easily be self-deceived into thinking that a mere label is an articulatory recipe. If a purported description is actually an articulatory one, and not an imitation label only, other persons by following the directions given and fulfilling all the conditions of articulatory movement should be able to produce the sound described without having heard it. This test is to some extent conditioned by the ability of the persons attempting to make the sound; for example, if they understand that the larynx needs to be lowered for a certain sound but do not know how to accomplish that movement, even a perfectly clear and accurate description of an implosive may not enable them to attain mastery

[65] Cf. the objection of Bloomfield (84–85) to phonetic rather than phonemic transcriptions.

of the sound — they first need instruction in methods of accomplishing this movement.

I applied this criterion to Ganthony's description of the " Ventriloquial Drone," in regard to which he says, " The acquirement of the ' Drone ' is the acquirement of all distant sounds." [66] He directs one to take a deep breath, to hold it while making a " retching sound at the back of the throat as though trying to be sick," to utter a prolonged " ah," exhaling slowly; this first will give a " grunt," then " a drone," a " sustained clear hum." [67] I tried to follow directions; result: retching sound, grunt, hum could all be made (by imitation-label technic from memory of such sounds), but nothing emerged which sounded particularly distant. Presumably, his discussion was an imitation label, not an accurate articulatory description. It seems very probable that the articulatory factor which Ganthony was trying to describe was a specific kind of glottal tension, and, further, that voice teachers must train pupils in a diametrically opposite direction to relax and enlarge the throat.

An interesting study might be made of deaf-mutes learning to speak. I attended several lectures of a class on lip reading to see what phonetic factors would emerge. Of course, books on the subject [68] use the articulatory method. Teaching deaf-mutes to speak — no matter how imperfectly — is a decided achievement for such an approach. The fact that deaf-mutes do not speak normally shows that for perfect success the articulatory technic needs to be combined with auditory imitation; the descriptions of the sounds would then be combination articulation–imitation labels.

In an attempt to discover articulatory factors unknown to me and, if possible, to make a rough correlation between the terminology of voice training and that of my phonetic analysis, I attended a few beginners' singing classes. [69] I had opportunity both to hear the instructor criticize the students and to have her describe in her terms certain effects in singing that I deliberately produced by articulatory

---

[66] Ganthony, *Practical Ventriloquism* [3], 13.

[67] Ganthony, 12–13. Bergen (*How to Become a Ventriloquist*, 23) has a significantly related description wherein he speaks of the ventriloquial voice as being a " pinched voice," a " succession of grunts and groans," with (23, 102) " pressure on the vocal cords."

[68] See Kinzie and Kinzie, *Lip-Reading*.

[69] The classes were held in Santa Ana Junior College.

methods with which I had previously experimented. Unfortunately I had too little time to make more than a few brief observations, but they are of interest in this connection.

When (according to my analysis) I deliberately restricted my pharynx by contracting it, or moving the tongue backward, I was told I had " failed to place the tone," or " was placing the tone at the back of my head " (instead of " between my eyes "). Similar analysis was reported when I gave marked lip unrounding or low back-tongue positions; more frequently these were called " spreading the tone." The instructor approved of my " rounded tone " when lips were rounded and vowels shaded toward high and front positions and when the back part of the tongue was raised (more than is my natural habit) as much as was consistent with producing the vowel concerned. A raucous sound made by raising the larynx, and with pharyngeal constriction marked especially by the approximation of the faucal pillars (rather than by the tongue approximating the back wall of the pharynx as in the pharyngeal-constriction type first mentioned), was also " spreading the tone." A marked lowering of the larynx was " tightening " the throat. Failure to give proper oral rounding, fronting, and the like, as well as the slightest suspicion of glottal friction added to the voicing, was " letting air out around the tone." Any constriction of the pharynx or tension of the muscles around the vocal cords was immediately noted and reproved. A deliberate lowering of the velum to cause excessive nasalization was due to the fact that I had " closed the turbinates, the small entrances to the sinuses."

The pupils were told to " put more [o] " in a sound to round it further. They were constantly instructed to " think the tone; you can think it wherever you want to." They were directed to " think the tone higher " to keep from flatting.

One of the consequences which surprised me most centered about such suggestions. I had supposed that by following strict articulatory procedure, deliberately shifting tongue or larynx here and there to get certain effects, no such " thinking " or " feeling " would be the result. On the contrary, even in the short time in which I tried to apply the technic, certain of these feelings of " placing the tone between the eyes," " feeling nothing between the diaphragm and the eyes," and the like, became quite real.

Presumably statements in textbooks such as those directing a person to do " anything to bring the voice out of the throat " [70] and to say so and so, " trying to aim the voice toward the hard palate just above the upper teeth " [71] (so as to " help to produce a vibrant, ringing quality in the tone ") are labels relating to relaxation and enlargement of the throat,[72] which in turn permit the feelings to be obtained.

Since directions for beginners' singing are accompanied by the living example of the teacher demonstrating both desired and undesired effects, while many of the apparently articulatory directions are innately impossible of prosecution, one draws the conclusion that music teachers use predominantly an imitation-label technic.

Such a procedure is valid, in spite of the objection a phonetician may at first have to it. After all, results are the essential thing, and if an impressionistic description gives phonetically strange labels to the items involved, that is immaterial within the imitation-label procedure provided students can be taught to sing. The discussion of the development of such feelings as have been mentioned above is a psychological problem with which I find myself unable to cope as a phonetician.

Even stronger arguments may be adduced for the validity of the imitation-label procedure, in music, because of the limitations of the articulatory technic itself. Not even the most ardent advocate of articulatory methods in phonetic instruction would attempt to teach a voice student to raise a note an octave by saying, " Make the vocal cords open and close just twice as fast."

This signalizes one of the basic limitations of articulatory phonetics. Prosody cannot be described satisfactorily by the articulatory technic. Relative acoustic judgments must be used instead.

The question should be faced as to why voice instructors employ an articulatory approach for mouth formations of vowels and consonants as little as they appear to. They are using an articulatory method to a very minor extent when they give exercises for flexibility

[70] Karr, *Your Speaking Voice*, 154 (quoting Skinner).
[71] Karr, 132.
[72] Karr, 119–30. Since writing this material I have seen Bartholomew's " Physical Definition of Good Voice Quality in the Male Voice," *Journ. Acoust. Soc. Am.*, 6 (1931), 25–33; in this excellent article Bartholomew discusses additional features. See also *idem, Acoustics of Music*, 139–59.

of the lips [73] and the like, but that hardly seems to exhaust its potential utility. Perhaps they are afraid that consciousness of mouth formations will eventually hinder the singing. That particular argument does not appear unanswerable to a phonetician. He knows perfectly well [74] that even a conscious, awkward, slow approach to a foreign language by conscious movements gains a closer approximation to the native sounds, and ultimately a freer conversational style, than can ever be attained (by an adult) by pure imitation. In as much as learning to make the voice pleasant is (for most of us) essentially the same as learning the sounds of a foreign language, phoneticians would not be unduly concerned at the consciousness, knowing that this tends to disappear with usage. Much of it has to disappear, inevitably, since it is manifestly physically impossible to think of perhaps two movements or positions for each of, say, three sounds per syllable at five syllables per second.[75] The same would be true of singing. Although there is a possibility that a few of the total articulatory movements might hang over in the consciousness longer than others and cause considerable trouble, it appears very doubtful that such a residue should of itself cause abandonment of the technic.

The real reason that voice teachers cannot use an articulatory approach for more of their problems is that none is provided by the phoneticians. The chief concern of the vocalist lies with the throat, and not with the mouth. Yet in all the literature I have seen hardly one single constructive pedagogical suggestion was given for making sounds in the pharynx,[76] for expanding or contracting the pharynx, releasing tension on vocal cords, and the like. No articulatory study of the throat remotely attempts to answer the needs of the vocalist. Why?

With very rare exceptions (of which Arabic has a few), things happening in the pharynx do not change phonemes. The norms established by phoneticians have excluded from detailed investigation almost everything which does not represent central distinguishing features in phonemic systems at large. The vocalist, on the other hand,

[73] See Karr, 130.
[74] See Jones, *Outline*, § 25; Noël-Armfield, 1; Sweet, 27.
[75] See Jones, *Outline*, § 43 (for numbers of syllables per second).
[76] See n. 41.

is seldom concerned with phonemic values, perhaps preferring to eliminate some contrast rather than spoil a beautiful tone; his concern is with nonphonemic factors almost exclusively, factors which have met with little or no discussion and for the teaching of which few pedagogical devices have been provided. Only when phoneticians take a larger view of their field and try to classify, study, and find ways of teaching all sounds, regardless of their " practical " value, only when they enter a realm a bit more like that of the pure science of the physicist, can they hope to discover data which eventually can provide vocal instructors with the procedures they need. Until then these instructors do well to retain tones " made between the eyes."

Doke says, " At the risk of appearing, to some, to be too pedantically minute in this phonetic study, I have decided to record in all my examples every phonetic phenomenon which presents itself. I shall leave nothing to deduction. For example, it will be found that [n] before [z] always implies the presence of [d] between them; I shall write [ndz]." [77] He believes, therefore, that his description embodies a purely articulatory approach, with no mixture of imitation-label technic.

This feeling of completeness is illusory, wherever found. In the [n] which he mentions, what is the position of the back part of the tongue? of the root of the tongue? of the epiglottis, the faucal pillars, pharyngeal wall? of the cheeks, the jaw, and entrance to the esophagus? how long was the sound held, and with what pitch and intensity? what type of transitional sounds did it have before and after it? Bloomfield well says of a phonetician, "Even his most ' exact ' record is bound to ignore innumerable nondistinctive features of sound." [78]

In proportion to his assumption of normal conditions, or his ignoring of certain moveable parts of the vocal apparatus, the phonetician inevitably uses imitation-label technic. This remains none the less true even when some parts of his description represent acceptable articulatory technic. As regards certain of the components, the description (or letter of the alphabet) is an articulatory label; as regards others it serves simultaneously as an imitation label, demanding a standard to prevent the sound from being spoken with an " accent."

[77] Doke, 5.   [78] Bloomfield, 84.

Sounds within the throat [79] are most often subsumed in this manner. Jespersen [80] states that a number of such articulatory minutiae probably need not be considered in certain sounds; some of these find no place in his analphabetic system.

Further evidence of imitation-label influence in phonetics appears in vowel description. The highest part of the tongue (or the closest) is generally chosen as the most useful classification peg.[81] That this is only a rough classification, for convenience, writers frankly admit, mentioning other factors which affect vowel quality too slightly (or nonphonemically) to be worth including. Such factors may be the position of the tongue tip,[82] the height of the jaw (which governs the amount of tongue recording on a palatogram),[83] the slope of the tongue,[84] the cheeks,[85] and so on. Russell makes a justifiable objection to the vowel-triangle [86] theory, partly because of these and similar factors. Although some differences in vowel production might prove to be below the threshold of perception (and hence might appear to result in the " same " vowel, and be legitimately classed together for that reason), others may prove to differ in ways which are seldom phonemic, and these can conveniently be subsumed under the (only approximately accurate) articulatory labels which are applicable within limits of broad production, but which require that imitation be added for a reproduction which is more like the model. The vowel

---

[79] For references see n. 41. Certain of the qualities of resonance, such as " metallic sound," mentioned by Bloomfield (94–95), may prove to be caused by such factors. Cf. Muckey, 85; see also Passy, *Sounds*, 20–21, where lowering of the larynx is said to give sepulchral voice. Perhaps here also are some of the elements which make people's voices different, so we can recognize them (Bloomfield, 76), so far as such individual characteristics are not caused by differences in the vocal mechanisms themselves. That many of these factors are not physiologically predetermined is evidenced by the fact that one person can mimic another. See also n. 67.

[80] Jespersen, *Articulations*, 10.

[81] See Grandgent, *German and English Sounds*, 11; Jespersen, *Articulations*, 18–19; Jones, *Outline*, §§ 48, 151; Kenyon, 64; Noël-Armfield, 31; *Passy, Sounds*, 57.

[82] Jones, *Outline*, § 124.

[83] Jespersen, *Articulations*, 11; Jones, *Outline*, § 128.

[84] Sweet, 15–16.

[85] Jespersen, *Articulations*, 10; Kenyon, 65.

[86] Russell, *Speech and Voice*, 77–83; idem, *The Vowel*, 133–56, 245–81, 282–304, 317–51, also *Proceedings of the Second International Congress of Phonetic Sciences* (1936), 198–205.

triangle, then, is seen to be a group of handy articulation–imitation labels; in common with the majority of other phonetic descriptions the most prominent and the roughly accurate adjustments find representation in articulatory statements, while the remainder are subsumed under the same tag in its secondary and simultaneous function for the imitation-label technic.

Additional evidence that such labels are not purely articulatory is seen in statements by Jones: " The value of the cardinal vowels cannot be learnt from written descriptions: they should be learnt by oral instruction from a teacher who knows them." [87] " The sound [ɔ] is best acquired by imitation, while observing carefully the position of the lips." [88] One of the functions of a teacher is " to act as a model of pronunciation." [89]

Noël-Armfield says that " No verbal description of any sound met with in language will enable the student to reproduce it exactly." [90] Jones states excellently the relation of articulatory and imitation technics for rougher and finer adjustments respectively.[91]

One might be tempted to conclude that all phonetic descriptions of sounds are arbitrary and invalid because certain features are included and others overlooked or subsumed in the label. Bloomfield objects to " exact " phonetic records as selecting details for description by " accidental and personal factors." [92] His chief complaint (amply justified) in regard to a phonetic transcription is its inconsistency, but he has " no objection to a linguist's describing all the acoustic features he can hear, provided he does not confuse these with the phonemic features." [93]

I believe it is possible, however, to find a method of dividing a sequence of sounds into nonarbitrary segments which are independent

[87] Jones, *Outline*, § 140.
[88] *Ibid.*, § 309.
[89] *Ibid.*, §§ 45, 47.
[90] Noël-Armfield, author's Preface.
[91] Jones, *Outline*, § 105: " This does not mean that the learner is expected to acquire vowels by ' simple imitation.' On the contrary, he will find a knowledge of the organic formation of vowels of considerable use to him. But this knowledge is not in itself sufficient. The finer adjustments of the tongue have to be done by means of sensory control from the ear." In addition to " adjustments of the tongue," Jones should have mentioned adjustments of other parts as well, such as the pharynx.
[92] Bloomfield, 84.
[93] *Ibid.*

of phonemes (see Chapter III and pp. 107–20) and then to choose, rationally, certain basic factors to be described for each of these sounds which would place it as a member of some general production type, giving a clue as to its air mechanisms and chambers, primary strictures, and so on (see pp. 151–56). Such a description would make no pretense at being complete, since it would be circumscribed by known limitations of the articulatory technic and by unavoidable perceptual variations. When the linguistically distinctive nature of certain sound features has been called to the attention of the phonetician, he can add those items which have been omitted by design (since they are phonetic minutiae) or by oversight (due to lack of training in that particular item) if they are pertinent to the descriptive project in hand. The initial classification would be designed to provide a relatively stable starting point for descriptive studies of various kinds — not at all a complete statement of the entire gamut of articulatory processes involved — and give a means for the abstract phonetic comparison of sounds in their major articulatory (not phonemic) structural features.

The articulatory technic and its analysis of marginal sounds are helpful in teaching. Students find it difficult to learn isolated facts and data which do not fit a system. The late Dr. Edward Sapir applied this principle to phonetics when he said that it was easier for a student to learn five hundred new sounds than five [94] (e.g. a student may find it difficult to make a voiceless lateral spirant, a " Welsh [l]," if he has had no training in the unvoicing of known sounds, but if the student has acquired the general method of unvoicing any sound whatsoever, he can readily produce dozens of voiceless sounds which he has never heard, including the lateral continuant, because they fit a pattern). Many sounds of speech can only be seen in a system when they are compared with marginal and nonspeech sounds; an articulatory classification best answers this need. Even lectures or books dealing with the phonemics of a single language might well profit by such a brief orientation.

Teachers of esophageal speech [95] to laryngectomized patients

---

[94] Dr. Sapir made the statement at Ann Arbor, in 1937, in a lecture to the Linguistic Institute.

[95] Cf. Jackson, " The Voice after Direct Laryngoscopic Operations, Laryngofissure and Laryngectomy," *Arch. of Otolaryngol.*, 31 (1940), 23–36; Levin, " Speech following Total Laryngectomy (without the Aid of the Mechanical

would benefit by a study of pharyngeal and oral air mechanisms, since they appear to be confused by these factors. On the one hand they deprecate any resort to " buccal whispers " [96] (which apparently come from these two mechanisms), whereas they seem to encourage beginners to use pharynx-air affricates in the first word that they are taught.[97] The more expert speakers do not employ these sounds for stops or affricates, but utilize esophageal air exclusively.[98]

The *instrumental articulatory technic,* the second of the four descriptive technics to be discussed,[99] is of especial value in measuring movements and positions to define precisely classifications presented by the auditory approach. Palatograms,[100] for example, clarify points of contact of the tongue in various sounds; X rays show the height and shape of tongue formation (primarily for vowels [101]); and so on.

The technic seems to be incapable of making a complete, significant classification independent of an auditory approach. For one thing, the strictures which it measures have varying functions in sound production (e.g. of causing vibrations; of controlling the direction of the air stream, as during nasal closure within oral sounds; of causing friction; and the like; see pp. 56–65, 129–36); measurement as such cannot classify these differences.

A second factor is one already mentioned (p. 15) — the perceptual thresholds of discrimination. Any classification of sounds as heard by the ear must take these thresholds into account, but instruments cannot find them without auditory checks.

But the technic here can be of great service to auditory phonetics

---

Larynx)," a paper read before the Northern Medical Society (Philadelphia, 1939); Morrison and Fineman, " Production of Pseudo-voice after Total Laryngectomy," *Trans. Am. Acad. Ophthalmol. and Otolaryngol.,* 41 (1936), 631–34; Schall, " Psychology of Laryngectomized Patients," *Arch. of Otolaryngol.,* 28 (1938), 581–84; Stetson, " Esophageal Speech for Any Laryngectomized Patient," *Arch. of Otolaryngol.,* 26 (1937), 132–42; *idem,* " Speech Movements in Action," *Trans. Am. Laryngol. Assn.,* 55 (1933), 29–42.

[96] See n. 95.

[97] See sound film prepared by Dr. N. M. Levin in collaboration with Dr. C. L. Jackson.

[98] See n. 97.

[99] The imitation-label technic (see pp. 16–18, 21–23) is not included in this group of four precisely because it does not describe items, but only labels them.

[100] See Jones, *Outline,* 79–81.

[101] See Noël-Armfield, 16–17; Russell, *The Vowel;* Parmenter and Treviño, " Vowel Positions as Shown by X–Rays," *Quart. Journ. Speech,* 18 (1932), 351.

by investigating the minimum movement or change of position which the ear can register. If, for example, the instrumentalist had experimentally classified such thresholds for minute vowel change as were caused respectively by tip of tongue in various positions, by root and other parts of the tongue, wall of pharynx, faucal pillars, height of larynx, height of jaw, cheeks (or, if necessary, if he had classified thresholds for combinations of such movements), then X rays of slightly different vowels (which the auditory approach said were different but could not analyze satisfactorily) could perhaps determine which changes of position caused the vowel changes and which could not have done so because they were below the perceptual level. Such investigations would help classify many items now subsumed by imitation-label technic under auditory articulation labels.

Furthermore, if, on the one hand, such perceptual thresholds of movement were classified, while a technic was provided for recording them, and, on the other, a suitable working theory were available for segmentation of strictural changes in a sequence, the instrumentalist could cut any continuum into perceptual phonetic units. For the need and possibility of such a postulation see Chapter III and pages 107–20.

In prosody, where the articulatory technic is weak, instrumental technic can make a considerable contribution. It can measure chest pulses [102] (for stress), photograph and time the movements of the vocal cords [103] (for pitch), and measure the length of time certain strictures are retained (for quantity). At present this can be done only imperfectly and within strict limits upon the sounds the technic can investigate (photographing the vocal cords, for example, seems for the present to be limited to certain vowels).

One might try to classify sounds by the *auditory acoustic technic,* the third descriptive method, and give labels to different types of tone quality as perceived by the ear. I have seen no attempt to do this systematically, and I personally can imagine no such terminology which would be as convenient as the articulatory type; it would probably develop almost strictly into an imitation-label technic (since the standards of sound which the labels represented would have to

[102] See Haden, *The Physiology of French Consonant Changes* (Supplement to *Language,* Dissertation 26), 19; Stetson, "Speech Movements in Action," *Trans. Am. Laryngol. Assn.,* 55 (1933), 29–42.

[103] See Herriott, "High Speed Motion Picture Photography," *Bell System Tech. Journ.,* 17 (1938), 393–405.

be established almost exclusively by samples, and the necessity of samples ultimately implies imitation for their production).

Jespersen's statement fifty years ago still seems applicable, " Not even the most ardent adherents of the ' acoustic ' point of view have ever tried to base their phonetic terminology or any system of notation on the acoustic properties of those sounds." [104] The acoustic criterion of the presence or the absence of audible friction, however, is one of the most basic to phonetics, especially in consonant–vowel distinctions (see p. 70–72) and gives a valuable supplement to articulatory descriptions. Sonority likewise has had influence on phonetic classifications (see pp. 69–70). Harris has mentioned that differences exist in consonant and vowel treatment based on articulatory versus acoustic descriptions.[105]

The auditory acoustic technic fills an exceedingly important place in the linguistic analysis of prosody; neither of the articulatory technics can handle the problem satisfactorily. The untrained person makes judgments of pitch, stress, and quantity by auditory acoustics. His are judgments relative to a vague standard or norm for a particular individual or community (" a low, soft, drawling voice ").

The trained musician can estimate much closer to fixed pitches or quantities. As with segmental sounds, presumably many more pitch differentiations can be perceived when contiguous (Fletcher states that there may be up to 2000 perceptible gradations from highest to lowest audible pitch [106]) than when noncontiguous.[107] Even when a subject attempts to retain pitch and quantity at certain levels he is unable to do so; variation occurs, especially in quantity.[108] Presumably much of this variation is below the threshold of perception.

The phonemicist makes relative acoustic judgments as regards contiguous or noncontiguous sounds in a phrase. The ear of a native speaker of a tone language registers this type of acoustic data (tones are " high " or " low " relative to each other, rather than to an

[104] Jespersen, *Articulations*, 3.

[105] Harris, Review of " Foundations of Language," by L. H. Gray, *Lang.*, 16 (1940), 229.

[106] Fletcher, *Speech and Hearing*, 162.

[107] The violinist, for example, in tuning his instrument immediately knows whether he is correct if the piano is struck, but he might be in error if he tried to tune merely by auditory memory of the note.

[108] Cf. Shohara.

absolute pitch; changing the key, i.e. all the pitches, does not change
tone; a single, level, isolated tone is not subject to classification — it
must be put next to others to see if it is relatively low or high, and
so on).[109] Similarly, the musician can sing " do, mi, sol, do " in any
key or octave, but retains the same intervals; speech differs primarily
in that linguistic pitch intervals are not strictly fixed, but vary freely
within certain limits or under certain fixed conditions, and the whole
key is readily changed between (or even in the middle of) phrases.
Some African tone languages transfer their somewhat flexible tone
intervals to musical instruments of a few fixed notes (pipes, drums,
and the like), for signalling.[110] It isn't too clear why persons who
readily " carry a tune " of a dozen or more relative pitches still find
it so difficult to learn a tone language of three or four.

The *instrumental acoustic technic,* the fourth descriptive method,
at present seems to make one of its greatest contributions in analyzing
prosody. Its accuracy goes infinitely beyond that of the auditory
approach. Interesting studies can thus be made of intonation and
prosodic factors which the auditory articulation technic cannot touch
(e.g. of certain emotional expressive states).[111] Right here lies its
greatest danger; whatever is more refined than the ear can record
becomes unsuitable for a phonetic classification.

Apart from this phonetic difficulty, linguistic studies suffer by
overdifferentiation of tone in tone languages, where tonemic studies
(i.e. phonemic statements of tone) are the only ones pertinent to linguistic structure. This may be the case even when phonographs and
similar devices are used to supplement auditory acoustic analysis.
Doke, for example, used a dictaphone for " careful analysis of sound
and tone, when reproduced repeatedly." [112] Result: nine registers,

[109] For brief suggestions for control of the variable factor in analysis of
prosodic systems see Pike, *Phonemic Work Sheet.*

[110] See Von Hornbostel, " African Negro Music," *Africa,* 1 (1928), 30–62.
For linguistic tone affected by use of words in singing see Herzog, " Speech Melody
and Primitive Music," *Musical Quarterly,* 20 (1934), 452–66.

[111] Expression of fear, anger, love, hate, and other emotions is, apart from
a few interjections, of a prosodic type superimposed on speech. As such it is not
readily susceptible to auditory articulation analysis. For an excellent instrumental
study see Fairbanks and Pronovost, " An Experimental Study of the Pitch Characteristics of the Voice during the Expression of the Emotions," *Speech Monographs,* 6 (1939), 87–104.

[112] Doke, 8.

which were nonphonemic or so unimportant that he was able to give permission of Westermann and Ward [113] to reduce the number greatly for a rough translation into their system of tone marking. Had each of these registers been phonemic, this reduction would be comparable to eliminating [p], [t], and [k] from English for a like orthographical reason.

Beach, working with similar means, says, " As far as *height* of tone is concerned, most writers on intonation have contented themselves with three degrees, which they call high, low, mid. Such simplicity is probably both adequate and desirable in any tonetic system consisting of only a few tones. I shall find it sufficient in my description of the *inherent tone* of strong roots in Hottentot. But it is altogether inadequate if one wishes to show the exact intonation of a sizable piece of connected speech." [114]

At the same time that such methods add too many tones, they tend to fix utterances in such a way that the normal free variation of the individual is lost.[115] This hinders phonemic analysis, since two levels of pitch which are everywhere freely interchangeable are to be equated as phonemically identical. When one repeatedly plays back a recording he hears none of this variation which would normally be present.

A similar danger exists when the acoustician studies, in segmental phonemes, differences that are below the perceptual threshold. Twaddell criticizes Bloomfield's phonemic discussion by saying: " That we do not find any such constant characteristic factor is of course a commonplace of experimental phonetics." [116] This very commonplace becomes dangerous when it unwarrantably implies or states that no two sounds are alike. For the ear they must be alike if the ear itself is physiologically incapable of telling them apart.

The instrumental acoustic technic can be of great value in finding perceptual thresholds of the ear in response to differing sound waves. This should aid in establishing a basis for the limitation of refinement

[113] Westermann and Ward, 202 n.

[114] Beach, 126.

[115] Beach (150–77) uses four recordings of the same material for analysis, with three different speakers, one of whom gives the story twice. This is decidedly helpful but fails to avoid the basic dangers.

[116] Twaddell, *On Defining the Phoneme* (*Language Monographs*, Vol. 16), 25.

of phonetic units (see p. 45) or alphabets; it is useless, for example, for an observer to use an alphabet more detailed than sounds he can hear, since there will be nonsystematic and nonsignificant variation in choice of symbols. Interesting studies can be made of acoustic phenomena which occur below the perceptual level, and even subjective phenomena (things " heard " which are not in the sound waves) can be added to objective data (e.g. a subjective intensity vibrato can be added to an objective frequency vibrato [117]).

Presumably the acoustician will ultimately have his own basic segmental units of sound. Actually, he seems to start with an articulatory unit.[118] He lacks also a significant classification for the study of linguistic structure and any system of phonetic transcription. Speaking of present limitations of the instrumental approach, Bloomfield says, " In fact, the laboratory phonetician usually knows, from other sources, the phonemic character of the speech-sounds he is studying; he usually formulates his problems not in purely acoustic terms, but rather in terms which he has borrowed from practical phonetics." [119]

Not all types of possible vocal sounds occur in speech. The acoustician is obviously limited to material which he finds in speech or interjections of various kinds; if he wishes to postulate sounds with which he has no contact, in order to contrast total possibilities with actual sounds of speech, he must postulate and produce them by articulatory analogies. Furthermore, if such limitations in the total of speech sounds prove to be due to articulatory factors, as seems likely (e.g. belches are not woven into normal speech presumably because of the articulatory difficulty of getting air with sufficient ease and speed to fix them into a stream of speech), then he could never discover this fact by a study of sound waves of speech.

[117] See Kock, " Certain Subjective Phenomena Accompanying a Frequency Vibrato," *Journ. Acoust. Soc. Am.*, 8 (1936), 23–25. See also Snow, " Change of Pitch with Loudness at Low Frequencies," *Journ. Acoust. Soc. Am.*, 8 (1936), 14–19. Snow found that with certain low sounds, the louder they were made, the lower the pitch seemed to the observers (sometimes as much as fifty per cent lower), even though the pitch actually remained stationary. Observers had general, but not perfect, agreement.

[118] See de Groot, " Instrumental Phonetics. Its Value for Linguists," *K. Akademie van Wetenschappen, Afdeelingen Letterkunde, Mededeelingen, 65*, A. 2 (1928), 48.

[119] Bloomfield, 85.

No classification of sound waves at present remotely approaches articulatory technic in pedagogical aids for the teaching of sounds.

Phonograph records can substitute for the instructor in phonetics in his capacity as a model,[120] where the imitation-label technic overlaps the articulatory one. Perhaps photographs of waves from a cathode ray tube may sometime serve a similar purpose as a test of the success of imitation.

In this chapter we have seen that phonetic systems have not been based upon the total number of sounds which are known to occur in speech. Unless consonant sounds are made with air coming out from the lungs and vowels are voiced, sounds fail to enter the main stream of phonetic inquiry and delineation, but are shunted into an obscure backwash of classification. For the investigation of these marginal types the writer has chosen to use an auditory analysis with description in terms of articulatory movements supplemented by a few acoustic criteria.

Auditory analysis is essential to phonetic study since the ear can register all those features of sound waves, and only those features, which are above the threshold of audibility and therefore available to any speech community, whereas analysis by instruments must always be checked against auditory reaction because it has no criterion apart from judgments of the ear to indicate what movements or features of sound waves are below the threshold of perception. Description based on movements of the vocal apparatus, even though supplemented by acoustic terms, is more convenient than description rendered entirely by means of auditory acoustic judgments, since the latter lacks sufficient points of reference which can be defined without the necessity of establishing them in relation to standards that can be duplicated only by imitation. In the following chapter further sound types will be discussed, ones which find even less place in phonetic literature than do the marginal sounds mentioned thus far.

[120] See Jones, *Outline*, §§ 47, 48.

CHAPTER II

NONSPEECH SOUNDS

NONSPEECH sounds [1] as produced by the human vocal apparatus [2] are mentioned in books on phonetics in various connections. In none have they been given treatment to indicate their importance for and bearing upon phonetic theory of speech or the classification of vocal sounds as a whole. This can hardly cause surprise since they are one step further removed from the speech norms that have been established (pp. 5–12) than are the marginal sounds, which have also been neglected. Their chief usage is for illustration of various types of sounds.

When an author discusses a sound type for which he finds no illustration in the phonemic norms of language, or which is used only in the phonemic norms of languages far removed from those with which his readers are likely to be acquainted, he may illustrate it with a nonspeech sound. Types requiring an inverse air stream (suction sounds), whether sounds inbreathed to the lungs or inverse to the mouth, may be illustrated by sounds of pain,[3] drinking,[4] pleasure,[5]

---

[1] The term is subject to flexible usage in this paper, without strict delineation. It may include sounds which do not occur in languages known to a particular author, sounds produced in cultural contexts other than speech (even if similar sounds occur in language), or even sounds thought to occur in speech only as rare variants of phonemes.

[2] No animal calls or the like are considered. Negus (*The Mechanism of the Larynx*) has interesting descriptions of the sound-producing mechanisms of a great many animals; see especially his Appendix No. 2. Neither are any possible parallels of human to animal sounds considered. The naïve thesis of Luthy (in his book *The Human Speech Sounds*, 1) will hardly find acceptance; five English vowels (which are also " common to the voices of all mankind — from Hottentot to German ") are said to be the fundamental sounds of the universe (and from these he develops his theory of consonants) as " proved " by the fact that they are identical with the vowels of " [mēääou]," " as uttered by the cat " in this " natural order."

[3] See Catford, " On the Classification of Stop Consonants," *Le Maître Phonétique*, 3d Series, 65 (1939), 5; Noël-Armfield, *General Phonetics* [4], 120; Passy, *The Sounds of the French Language*, 86; Sweet, *A Primer of Phonetics* [3], 43.

[4] See Sweet, 43.

[5] See Noël-Armfield, 120; Passy, 86.

kissing,[6] surprised commiseration,[7] impatience,[8] or by a signal to urge horses,[9] and the like.

Types of movements may likewise be demonstrated even if unknown in speech as such; lip trills for guiding horses are an example.[10]

Nonspeech sounds are sometimes employed as analogies in describing well-known speech sounds. A cough is frequently used to illustrate a glottal stop; [11] the sound made by blowing out a candle, to illustrate some type of bilabial voiceless spirant; [12] a puff of breath, for aspiration.[13] A rarer expedient is a sound of surprise to demonstrate increasing force of breath pulse.[14]

A few nonspeech sounds are used as approaches to exercise for the attainment of some phonetic skill; this type may be seen in the practice of yawning to gain control of the velum.[15]

Occasionally abnormal conditions of the speech mechanism are mentioned and illustrated by resultant sounds — bronchial rattling, and snorting or sniffling,[16] for example.

Apart from exemplifying speech sounds by showing the manner of their production, nonspeech sounds may be used to clarify the application of a phonetic alphabet. Bell, to demonstrate his " visible speech," listed and wrote with his symbols many nonspeech sounds, many more than can be found elsewhere. From his long list [17] one may mention the " interjectional or inarticulate utterances " of sighing, panting, fluttering, shuddering, sobbing; the sneer, yawn, gasp, hiccough, pang, moan; the murmur of ridicule, vexation, disgust; and so on.

[6] See Passy, 87; Sweet, 43.

[7] See Bloomfield, *Language*, 94.

[8] See Passy, 87.

[9] See Bloomfield, 94; Noël-Armfield, 121; Passy, *Sounds*, 87.

[10] See Noël-Armfield, 8.

[11] See Forchhammer, *How to Learn Danish* [4], 1; Jones, *An Outline of English Phonetics* [4], 554; Ripman, *Elements of Phonetics*, 6; Sweet, 12; Viëtor, *German Pronunciation*, 59.

[12] See Jones, § 685; Kenyon, *American Pronunciation* [6], 126; Noël-Armfield, 86; Westermann and Ward, *Practical Phonetics for Students of African Languages*, 18.

[13] See Bloomfield, 82; Jones, § 497; Jones and Woo, *A Cantonese Phonetic Reader*, xi; Kenyon, 32; Noël-Armfield, 59.

[14] See Sweet, 48.

[15] See Westermann and Ward, 16.

[16] See Noël-Armfield, 5.

[17] Bell, *Visible Speech* (Inaugural Ed.), 50.

Two writers suggest several nonspeech sounds which their students are to use for practicing analysis of sounds and their transcription. Noël-Armfield's " peculiar noises " [18] and Krapp's " sounds not used in articulate speech " [19] are quite similar to each other and to part of Bell's list.

Krapp [20] and Noël-Armfield [21] employ a few nonspeech sounds to show a contrast with speech sounds. Sapir [22] has a discussion of the psychological and functional difference between the sound of candle blowing and the speech unit [hw]. Bloomfield mentions the difference in the interpretation of the sound of glottal stop by speakers of a language in which it is a phoneme and by foreign listeners who are trained not to respond to a " catch in the throat." [23]

Passy has a rare type of entry for a nonspeech sound when he includes whistles among " accessory " sounds because they are " sometimes used to convey meaning." [24] Other vocal expressive devices he ignores.

Many writers,[25] especially those describing the phonetics of single languages, make no use of nonspeech sounds.

Klinghardt [26] emphasizes the importance of nonspeech sounds for phonetic theory. Unfortunately, he devotes attention to but a few such sounds (though he does discuss some nonspeech movements which illustrate the mechanism of certain sounds), and they do not lead him to depart in any marked degree from the customary type of classification.

Phoneticians, failing to recognize the broadness of the field which is legitimately and profitably theirs, usually start with the assumption

[18] Noël-Armfield, 180 (kiss, sniff, snort, hiccough).

[19] Krapp, *The Pronunciation of Standard English in America*, 143 (sigh, cough, cluck, click, sniff, ' hmph,' ' huh,' ' eh,' ' hm,' the sound of calling a cat, and the sound for starting horses).

[20] Krapp, 2.

[21] Noël-Armfield, 5.

[22] Sapir, " Sound Patterns in Language," *Lang.*, 1 (1925), 37–51.

[23] Bloomfield, 82.

[24] Passy, 88.

[25] Gairdner, *The Phonetics of Arabic;* Karlgren, *A Mandarin Phonetic Reader (Archives d'Études Orientales*, Vol. 13) ; Nicholson, *A Practical Introduction to French Phonetics;* Stirling, *The Pronunciation of Spanish;* Lowie, " Hidatsa Texts . . . ; with Grammatical Notes and Phonograph Transcriptions by Zellig Harris and C. F. Voegelin," *Prehistory Research Series*, I, No. 6 (1939), 183–84.

[26] Klinghardt, *Artikulations- und Hörübungen.*

that it does not include sounds apart from speech. The first sentence of Sweet's book states, " Phonetics is the science of speech-sounds." [27] Jones's *Outline of English Phonetics* begins: " The Nature of Speech. Spoken language consists of . . . ." [28] Passy says of speech, " The study of these sounds constitutes a science which we call *phonetics*." [29] Noël-Armfield appears to take a broader view when he remarks that phonetics " may be described as the science which deals with the gymnastics of the organs of speech, both in theory and in practice." [30] Practically, however, he abandons this position immediately, in so far as his own investigation is concerned, when he rules out of consideration various items which " cannot be classed as speech-sounds." [31]

Perhaps the reason for this assumption can be discovered in Sapir's discussion, which shows that sounds of phonetic systems function differently from similar sounds apart from such systems.[32] In regard to candle blowing as compared with [hw] he notes that the one has a separate function in the business of blowing, while the other is good only as a symbol in speech, with no meaning otherwise; the one can be varied to [ʃ] or [x], and so on (but may never be voiced), or have great variation in intensity, while the other has variants to voicing, [w], and is not so strongly articulated; the one has no associations and is not in a system, while the other is associated with other sounds in words and is one of a limited series of other sounds from which it essentially stands aloof.

This describes the speech sound according to its function; the phonetician should be able to describe a sound regardless of its function (and hence when it is not in speech); otherwise his phonemic description of one language essentially influences that of another, or sounds of phonemic systems are described in part by functional features which are essentially variable (as parts of differing systems), rather than by a more stable articulatory phonetic procedure.

The decision that a sound is to be included in general phonetic charts or classifications often rests upon the fact that it occurs frequently as a phonemic norm in speech, or as a variant of a norm; if it

[27] Sweet, 1.
[28] Jones, 1.
[29] Passy, *Sounds*, 5.
[30] Noël-Armfield, 1.
[31] Noël-Armfield, 6.
[32] Sapir, *op. cit.* in *Lang.*, 1 (1925), 37–51.

fails to find such usage, a sound tends to be omitted. The classification of laterals illustrates this. Never have I found a chart which included bilabial lateral sonorants as one of the basic types (although [f] is sometimes principally a lateral, actually occurring in speech [33]). Jones's handling of varieties of English [s] [34] demonstrates how nonphonemic variants are given a minor place, even when such sounds are known to appear. Because nonphonemic variants and nonspeech sounds are thus ignored or slighted, supposedly pure general phonetic classifications are actually cut down and tailored to fit an abstraction of phonemic patterns.

Unless the phonetician can predict that certain types will never occur in speech, he cannot afford to overlook them, lest his classification be incomplete and inaccurate; but he cannot make such a prediction until he has studied them — and perhaps not even then. No one seems to have attempted to work out a system of nonspeech sounds as distinct from speech types with this prediction in mind.

Perhaps such a study would show that certain types of nonspeech sounds are potential speech sounds, as evidenced by the fact that scattered members of related types have been found in language, while others are presumably ultimate nonspeech sounds, since no approximation of their general mechanism has ever come to light either as phonemic norm or variant.

Instead of making a study to determine the relationship, investigators appear to have postulated a sharp division between speech and nonspeech sounds, on insufficient evidence. Noël-Armfield mentions the difference, with a criterion which cannot be consistently applied. Speech sounds for him are " voluntary," and intentional. One of his illustrations of involuntary sound is the snore.[35] Yet what if the phonetician, or a boy in fun, voluntarily and intentionally produces a snore or some other nonspeech type such as a belch, or cough, or sigh — does that make it a speech sound when it does not occur in speech? Krapp says that breath expelled forcibly through the nose is " of course not an articulate speech sound. Articulate speech

---

[33] See Jones, § 693.

[34] Jones, § 709 and n.

[35] Noël-Armfield, 6. Noël-Armfield's other illustrations (5), taken from abnormal physical conditions (a cold producing bronchial rattle, sniffing, snorting), merely obscure the issue, which is concerned with sounds produced by persons in normal health.

sounds are only those sounds which are articulated, or joined to other sounds in formation of sound groups or words." [36] Yet sounds very similar to this, voiceless nasal spirants, occur as conditioned variants of [h] before nasals in Totonaco, Mazateco, Tlapaneco,[37] and many other languages.

If no criterion can ultimately be found of the difference between types of speech sounds and nonspeech sounds, then a phonetic classification must include them all. Otherwise, today's nonspeech sounds are potential speech sounds, and may tomorrow be found in some language to upset the incomplete classification. Sounds which are nonspeech from the point of view of one language may be phonemic in another (or even in the same one, as Sapir's illustration shows), and demand articulatory description.

Perhaps every phonetician has had an experience similar to mine, of postulating certain sounds, thinking they would never occur in speech, only to discover that they do so. I have found, for example, occasional bilateral bilabial sonorants as nonphonemic variants of the vowel [u] in Mixteco.[38] Such a discovery is even more surprising when the sound proves to be the phonemic norm.

In the earlier days of phonetic theory there was no opportunity to separate phonetics strictly from phonemics, simply because the latter was not understood. However, in spite of the development of phonemic study, which should presumably have caused the reëxamination of phonetic data, classifications remain essentially unchanged. Neither does there seem to be any discussion except Bell's where the author attempts to fit all nonspeech sounds known to him into his phonetic system. Those nonspeech sounds used for demonstrating speech sounds serve as pedagogical aids in the same way as do steam cylinders,[39] musical instruments,[40] the drawing of a cork from a bottle,[41] the use of a blowpipe,[42] and so on. Their purpose is illustrative, not analytical; the system remains the same as if they had been left unmentioned.

---

[36] Krapp, 2.
[37] Indian languages of Mexico.
[38] An Indian language of Mexico.
[39] See Catford, *op. cit.* in *Le Maître Phonétique,* 3d Series, 65 (1939), 4.
[40] See D. C. Miller, *The Science of Musical Sounds,* 23; Passy, *Sounds,* 2–5.
[41] See Miller, 22.
[42] See Bell, 62.

Even Bell's usage of nonspeech sounds was due more to a desire to show the universal application of his alphabet to speech than to a conviction that nonspeech sounds were basic to an understanding of phonetics. Although Bell's work is now over seventy years old, his list represents a more complete analysis than any other I have seen. Unfortunately, though he was reaching after the understanding of many types of sounds, his failure to grasp numerous basic features, such as the mechanism of clicks, glottalized sounds (ejectives), and others, together with the fact that his list is very incomplete and utterly without organization, makes the work of little value for new study.

Despite its being true that some sounds probably never have occurred nor will occur as phonemic norms, the phonetician interested in speech should not ignore them. They may provide the contrasting element which aids the appreciation of the highly selective nature of the majority of speech types.

Many phonetic factors (compare " Strictural Function," pp. 56–65) have passed without sufficient comment simply because incomplete data have hindered phoneticians from discovering the bias which those very data have engendered.

The discovery of even a few basically new mechanisms could produce thousands of shades of sound when they had been expanded in the light of present phonetic theory; additional thousands can be made by recombinations of elements already well known. The number of possible nonspeech sounds, as far as significantly new types are concerned, however, is not so limitless as might at first appear,[43] and any statement of the impracticability of studying them based upon such a premise proves to be invalid.

Makers of phonetic alphabets, apart from Bell, have chosen to limit their field to sound types that occur in speech. The International Phonetic Association has included only speech sounds in its alphabet.[44] Even Bloch and Trager, though they make certain marked advances in classification of sounds as a basis for their symbols (especially in regard to nonpulmonic mechanisms, following Catford) have seen fit to do likewise. Evidently, to them, nonspeech

---

[43] Cf. Krapp, 2.

[44] *The Principles of the International Phonetic Association*, Supplement to *Le Maître Phonétique* (1912); with chart revised to 1932.

sounds are not included in " phonetic material," since, even though they say that their system " is believed to be all-inclusive " [45] and " is intended to provide the widest possible range of devices for the recording of phonetic material," [46] no provision seems to be made for many sounds well known to them, some of which actually occur in types of communication. No devices are proposed which would, for example, give the full phonetic representation of the speech of a high school boy who whistles to get the attention of a friend, and replies with a " Bronx cheer " (the type which uses oral pressure and lip vibration) when the wrong person answers. Nor is there a basic sign to modify their symbols so they could record belched sounds (or the speech of a laryngectomized patient speaking with an air stream initiating in the esophagus rather than the lungs). When such sounds occur in connected speech they sometimes carry important social connotations,[47] and need symbols if complete representation is to be given.

As a background for this study I searched for types of nonspeech sounds in the phonetics books (whose material I have reviewed above) and other sources. In books on voice I found no discussion of nonspeech sounds, although Bender and Kleinfeld had in their exercises a number of nonspeech items.[48] Their analysis of sounds, however, cannot be trusted (witness their description of English [k], [g], and [n] as " palatal clicks " [49]), and their exercises are often proportionately unworkable.

A few helpful analyses of sounds resulting from some physical condition (hiccough, sneeze, cough, and the like) were found in medical literature.[50] The most important of such material was a group of articles on esophageal speech,[51] which might be considered a border

[45] Bloch and Trager, *Tables for a System of Phonetic Description* (Preliminary Ed.), 2.

[46] Bloch and Trager, 3.

[47] Says the host: " We (yawn) have had a lovely (yawn) evening." "(Burp)," replies the guest, " where's (hic) my hat ? "

[48] Bender and Kleinfeld, *Speech Correction Manual, Containing 317 Practical Drills for Speech and Voice Improvement.*

[49] Bender and Kleinfeld, 205.

[50] Cunningham, *Text-book of Anatomy* [17]; Gray, *Anatomy of the Human Body* [23]; Howell, *A Textbook of Physiology* [14]; Kimber, Gray, and Stackpole, *Textbook of Anatomy and Physiology* [10]; Negus; Stevens and Davis, *Hearing;* Travis, *Speech Pathology.*

[51] See pp. 24–25, n. 95.

line between speech and nonspeech types. Sounds which the normal, well person is physiologically incapable of producing I have not included in the classification in this text, nor have I investigated many sounds produced from abnormal conditions.

Other sounds were collected from scattered sources. Bell's list had most of those resulting from mental states.[52] A group of phonetic students were invited to make contributions for analysis. The sounds of a deaf-mute added an item or two. A young baby's babbling failed to offer more than one or two hints. A few types were obtained by trying to parallel by the voice sound-producing processes occurring in nature. A much more important source was a collection of my own sounds, recalled from earlier days, when they had been made in the carefree fashion mentioned by Sapir.[53]

The most important source of all was the deliberate effort to produce sounds postulated by analogy with known speech sounds, starting both from speech sounds and from clues given by nonspeech sounds; especial attention was given to speech sounds other than those produced with an egressive air stream from the lungs. One type which I am still trying to obtain, for example, is an implosive stop (suction created by lowering the larynx) voiced with ingressive rather than egressive air from the lungs.

The analysis of these sounds was by auditory articulation technic almost exclusively, although I took a few kymographic tracings which substantiated certain of my findings, and investigated some pharyngeal sounds by means of a dentist's mirror. On points where the auditory technic would not serve, I consulted various works on instrumental phonetics,[54] though these rarely concerned themselves with nonspeech sounds.

The instrumentalist should be able to profit by a study of a more complete phonetic classification than is at present available, since many items must creep into a gross acoustic record which are ignored by the phonetician, who can easily cut them from his record and

[52] Laughter, sighing, and the like. For fear, anger, and other emotions see p. 28, n. III.

[53] Sapir, *Language*, 46 n. "When we shout or grunt or otherwise allow our voices to take care of themselves as we are likely to do when alone in the country on a fine spring day, we are no longer fixing vocal adjustments by voluntary control. Under these circumstances we are almost certain to hit on speech sounds that we could never learn to control in actual speech."

[54] For books and articles see Bibliography.

hearing — or who, in fact, may hear them only with considerable difficulty and training — but which the acoustician would find harder to ignore since there is within the mechanical record no perceptual aid to label certain factors as " unimportant."

The value to the practical phonetician of the study of nonspeech sounds, apart from its specific contribution to the investigation of the demarcation of speech and nonspeech types, is similar to that of the study of marginal sounds: a broader classification is provided for pedagogy, and for the elimination of phonemic influence in phonetics, while a surer foundation is provided for researches into the differing functions of various parts of the mechanism, for the postulation of nonphonemic segmentation of continuums, and so on.

CHAPTER III

UNITS OF SOUND

SPEECH, as phoneticians well agree, consists of continuous streams of sound within breath groups; [1] neither sounds nor words are separated consistently from one another by pauses, but have to be abstracted from the continuum. Phonemicists concur in the belief that some unit of speech, the phoneme, can be discovered as the basic constituent of a linguistic system. Their agreement does not extend to the exact definition of such a unit, [2] but that is not pertinent to this study; no new definition is attempted.

A different problem is that which is here answered in the affirmative: Is there a significant halfway point between the continuum and the phoneme? Is there a real, nonfictitious segment of sound which is not a phonemic one?

Many writers actually work with a phonetic unit under the name " speech sound " or " phone." I have found no attempt to show the difference between a nonspeech sound and a speech sound as the starting point for such postulations of speech sound. This has already been discussed in Chapter II (pp. 35–38) and needs no further mention here.

Delineation of speech sounds has centered about two factors. The first of these represents an attempt to differentiate speech sounds from phonemes. [3]

Jones uses the term " speech sound " to mean one particular variant [4] of a phoneme that has " definite organic formation and definite

---

[1] See Bloomfield, *Language*, 76; Brøndal, " Sound and Phoneme," *Proceedings of the Second International Congress of Phonetic Sciences* (1936), 43; Jones, *An Outline of English Phonetics* [4], §§ 41, 1002–1006; Kenyon, *American Pronunciation*, 31–32; Noël-Armfield, *General Phonetics* [4], 57–58; Passy, *The Sounds of the French Language* [3], 23–28; Sweet, *A Primer of Phonetics* [3], 45.

[2] For a grouping of many definitions see Twaddell, *On Defining the Phoneme* (*Language Monographs*, Vol. 16). Twaddell himself (33) considers the phonemic unit to be fictitious.

[3] Jones, § 189. [4] Jones, §§ 193–99.

acoustic quality which is incapable of variation." [5] Thus the initial sounds of 'keep,' 'cool,' 'call,' are "three distinct sounds." [6]

Noël-Armfield at first glance appears to make a similar statement: "A speech-sound is an individual variety, whereas a phoneme is a family of individual varieties, which, as it were, cluster around a common centre, and is the name given to a number of sounds which are, from a scientific point of view, varieties of the same speech-sound, though these sounds are so alike acoustically that when in combination with other sounds the normal ear fails to detect any difference." [7] He illustrates by pointing out the difference between the initial sounds of 'kid' and 'cad,' and so on. But what is the basic unit of which he makes the speech sound an individual variety? He does not say, unless by "scientific point of view" he means a phonemic one, in which case "speech-sound" for him is identical with "phoneme" and varieties of each are to be equated.

The succeeding statement, "Different varieties of the same speech-sound may belong to one phoneme in one language, and in another to two phonemes," would substantiate such an interpretation, as would a statement elsewhere that the term "glide" may be applied, not only to a "necessary intermediate sound between two regular speech-sounds, but also to any sound leading up to or following any speech-sound represented by the ordinary spelling [sic]." [8]

Kenyon uses "speech sound" as equivalent to "phoneme": it is significant for identifying or distinguishing meanings; [9] it may be applied to a group of sounds varying because of phonetic surroundings; [10] the sound [h], even though occurring in a dialect, is not a speech sound if not distinctive. [11]

Sounds for Kenyon are neither phonemes nor speech sounds if they are not distinctive. This applies to the aspiration of stops in English [12] (but not to languages in which aspirated and unaspirated stops are phonemically different [13]) and to various types of nonsignificant transitions [14] (but not to phonemic glides [15]); a speech sound

---

[5] Jones, § 193.
[6] Jones, § 193.
[7] Noël-Armfield, 30.
[8] Noël-Armfield, 61.
[9] Kenyon, 32.
[10] Kenyon, 33.

[11] Kenyon, 141.
[12] Kenyon, 32, 50, 139.
[13] Kenyon, 32-33.
[14] Kenyon, 32.
[15] Cf. Kenyon, 59, 152-61, 233.

may be identical with a nonspeech sound which occurs in a different position in the same language [16] or in different languages.[17]

Kenyon also mentions the possibility of a different definition of " speech sound " from that which he regularly employs, in the sense of one definite position or movement of the speech organs. " In this sense, the [t] sounds in *till, still,* and *outdo* are different speech sounds." [18] This represents the start of an attempt to establish a unit between the continuum and the phoneme, but Kenyon does not develop it further.

A second attempt at the delineation of speech sounds (in addition to contrasting them with phonemes) consists in the effort to cut sounds from their continuums, to mark their borders, to isolate them from other sounds. This endeavor has brought into play more phonemic assumptions than the first one, and at present there seems to be available no consistent or useful manner of cutting the continuum apart from a linguistic (phonemic) division.

The definition of " speech sound " to mean variants of phonemes in particular contexts gives no aid whatsoever to this project, since the borders of such units are still phonemic, not phonetic, ones: the points at which the continuum is cut under such a procedure are those determined by the linguistic system, not by any innate phonetic features of the continuum.

Any phonetic (rather than phonemic) system of dividing a continuum into unit components must be just as applicable to a series of nonsense syllables as to some particular language. Any semantic, phonemic, linguistically distinctive criteria applied immediately make the unit invalid for analysis of phonetic structure per se.

Beach [19] states the problem precisely, then immediately slips into the use of phonemic criteria for an invalid solution: " The primary unit of phonetics is the speech-sound or phone . . . the difficulty [of describing that unit] lies in prescribing exactly what amounts of the chain of speech shall constitute single phones." " No definition has yet been devised which could be equally well applied to all languages. In English it is convenient to think of [nd] in *endeavor* as two phones

[16] Kenyon, 33.

[17] Kenyon, 84–85.

[18] Kenyon, 33. Compare the discussion above (pp. 42–43) of Jones's definition of speech sound.

[19] Beach, *The Phonetics of the Hottentot Language,* 29–30.

[n] plus [d]; in Zulu and Xhosa it is convenient to consider [nd] in *indoda* as a single phone." One readily sees that the criterion of " convenience " here is purely the phonemic status of the sounds concerned.

Some investigators state or imply that no consistent unit of sound can be found, other than the phoneme (and perhaps the syllable), which divides a continuum. Rather than that, the possible divisions are said to be infinite, with no logical stopping place between the phoneme and the continuum. Although Stetson asserts that a continuum can be divided phonetically into syllables by articulatory (and resultant acoustic) phenomena, he denies that a continuum can be divided into sounds — they " have no independent existence in speech." [20] Brøndal states, " A sound can be viewed as built up of any desired number of successive parts, whereas a phoneme is indivisible from the standpoint of a given language." [21] Bloomfield says that a speech utterance " can be viewed as consisting of any desired number of successive parts." [22] Other phoneticians maintain that a glide is composed of " infinitesimal intermediate positions," [23] even though these may be inaudible.

Some of these statements must be qualified in view of the necessity of recognition of perceptual units. If one kept cutting a continuum, one would run to the absurdity of trying to analyze one half of a sound wave. Only the instrumentalist can cut things so fine. The person dealing with vocal sounds as they register on the ear must limit himself to sounds within the threshold of perception of normal individuals. Anything too fast or consisting of too minute a change to be perceived cannot, by its very nature, be a phonetic unit from an auditory or speech standpoint.[24] This limits the number of units in any given sequence a very great deal. Only instrumental researches can decide exactly how much.

Even the best-trained phonetician, with the widest phonemic background, can hear but a limited number of sounds in a sequence.

[20] Stetson, *Motor Phonetics* (*Arch. Néer. Phon. Expér.*, Vol. 3), 33. See below, n. 63.

[21] Brøndal, 43.

[22] Bloomfield, 76.

[23] Sweet, 52. See also Passy, 88.

[24] Voiceless stops do not enter this category since their central phenomena are slow enough to register as lack of sound vibrations.

If different phoneticians, who have had different phonemic backgrounds, persist in hearing almost the identical number of " sounds," might it not be indicative that they are approaching the perceptual limit for rapid speech? If they are approaching such a limit, and find near agreement, may they not be approaching the recording of phonetic segments which are ultimately basic to phonemic units and which limit the possibilities of those units?

Several items contribute to the conclusion that there must ultimately be some such phonetic segmentation behind speech: The " very accurate " [25] transcriptions of phonetic experts differ but little from each other, or even from those of persons with slight phonetic training, when it comes to the total number of segments which they record for a given sequence. The differences occur primarily at what might be called *fluctuant segments* (or *fluctuants*) in phonemic–phonetic unit division: the fricative of homorganic affricates, " nasalized " stops, aspiration of various kinds, the glottal stop, and glides from one vocalic position to another. These fluctuants are difficult to hear in proportion to their grouping into single phonemes, or their lack of phonemicity, in the language of the observer. By far the largest number of disagreements of hearing and recording which the phoneticians would have among themselves lies in the realm of minute articulatory differences — points of articulation, degrees of articulation, and the like. These have practically no bearing on determining the number of segments which compose a sequence, but only upon the identification of one segment with another which is not contiguous to it, or its minute articulatory classification.

Alphabets reflect the same situation. They are designed to record approximately equal numbers of segments in a sequence, but add different types of diacritics for minutiae of an articulatory order. Bloomfield, commenting on the development of phonetic alphabets, remarks that their inventors meant their alphabets to be able to record every acoustic variety of sound in language, an aim which only a mechanical record could fulfill, and adds, " in practice, the phonemic principle somehow slipped in: usually one wrote a symbol for each phoneme, but these symbols were highly differentiated and cluttered up with diacritical marks, for the purpose of indicating ' exact ' acoustic values." [26] It appears extremely significant that a sharp

[25] Cf. Jones, § 568.   [26] Bloomfield, 87.

difference existed between the number of symbols in the sequence (even if by way of near-phonemic writing), and their complicated modification. Again, this points toward a basic and real division of any continuum into a specific number of segments; the description of these segments is what receives sharply varied representation.

One more factor contributes to the conviction that there must exist a phonetic segmentation more universal and fixed than the phonemic one: If a continuum represents a mere flow of sound with no points at which segmentation naturally occurs (according to Brøndal's statement [see p. 45] that it may be viewed as built up of any desired number of parts), how could it possibly have happened by chance that phonemic systems the world over cut such a continuum in almost identical places, except where the fluctuants are concerned? Even the very points where languages in their phonemic systems differ in establishing their phonemic borders, and the narrow range of sound types within which these differences occur, emphasize the fact that a universal segmentation lies behind vocal expression, and that in a certain few places this natural segmentation is not sufficiently sharp-cut to force all phonemic systems to make quite the same choice at those spots.

It follows, also, that a phonetic segmentation can be carried on with utility, if some consistent method can be found for classifying the fluctuants. It is precisely at these points that phoneticians allow phonemic influence to prevent such a classification, as will be seen in a moment.

Instrumentalists can in general cut sounds out of sequences, but Haden says they have difficulty in doing so unless there is a regular alternation of voiced and voiceless sounds.[27] De Groot remarks, " There can be little doubt that the current textbooks of phonetics scarcely trouble about giving a definition or a characterization of a speech-sound that might offer a starting point for experimental re-searches. In fact, I did not find an adequate definition in any one of them." [28] Since, as Bloomfield states, laboratory phoneticians

[27] Haden, *The Physiology of French Consonant Changes* (Supplement to *Language*, Dissertation 26), 16. See, however, Parmenter and Treviño, " The Length of the Sounds of a Middle Westerner," *Am. Speech*, 10 (1935), 128.

[28] De Groot, " Instrumental Phonetics. Its Value for Linguists," *K. Akademie van Wetenschappen, Afdeelingen Letterkunde, Mededeelingen*, 65, A. 2 (1928), 48.

usually formulate their problems in terms " borrowed from practical phonetics," [29] any clarification of the fluctuants should be of considerable aid. To be of most value to the instrumentalist such a definition must distinguish very carefully between the data of the sound waves and the perceptual elements registered by the ear.

Numerous investigators agree that speech sounds are made with the speech organs in positions which are fixed or practically fixed. Jones speaks of a " speech-sound proper " [30] as one of definite organic formation; he contrasts vowels with diphthongs, the former being produced with " approximately stationary " organs of speech, the latter with a " clearly perceptible movement." [31] Westermann and Ward state that a phone results from " one position of the organs of speech." [32] Sweet holds that " Analysis regards each sound as a fixed stationary point . . . analysis concerns itself only with the middle of the fully developed sound," [33] while flap consonants " are pure glides, organically as well as acoustically, there being absolutely no fixed point in their formation." [34] Kenyon says that in the phrase, ' the most of the time,' there are thirteen speech sounds and for each " the speech organs are momentarily in a definite position "; [35] since [u] implies fixed position of lips and tongue " for the duration of the vowel," [36] [w] cannot be [u] plus a vowel.

Perhaps fluid positions rather than fixed positions should be taken as the basis for a satisfactory theory of phonetic segments, since a fixed position would appear to be a departure from reality. Nevertheless, there may actually prove to be a sharp basic perceptual difference between sounds usually classified as fixed and certain ones (e.g. vowel glides) of the fluctuant type. Such a division may ultimately explain why fluctuant types are combined differently from the " fixed " types in various phonemic systems.

Jones [37] and Kenyon [38] both mention two kinds of sounds in speech: speech sounds (fixed, the phonemes) and glides (moving, the transitions). Both authors list as exceptions to their groupings the

[29] Bloomfield, 85.   [30] Jones, § 190.   [31] Jones, § 240.

[32] Westermann and Ward, *Practical Phonetics for Students of African Languages*, 28.

[33] Sweet, 44.   [36] Kenyon, 152.

[34] Sweet, 64.   [37] Jones, §§ 2–6, 102, 219.

[35] Kenyon, 32.   [38] Kenyon, 31–32, 33, 152–61.

vowel glides which make the " consonants " [w] and [j], and some of the diphthongs. These exceptions correspond directly to their phonemic interpretations of English, and nothing they advance counterbalances the strong implication that phonemics, not phonetic structure, has caused this change of classification. Though Jones speaks of most glides as " inevitable " and as being formed along " the most direct route " between speech sounds,[39] and contrasts them with " independent " vowel glides which are " expressly made " (rather than being the inevitable medium between other sounds), such a division is not convincing in view of the fact that the vowel glides " start in the position of one vowel and move in the direction of another ";[40] the audibility of the glide will not explain its independence, since, though " most glides are inaudible," at least some are " always clearly audible."[41]

If one cannot have consistent criteria for determining whether or not a glide is a separate sound, or part of a preceding or a following one, there remains no chance for consistent segmentation. If phonemic criteria are used, the division is valid only for phonemic purposes.

Passy says that " Glides are accessory sounds produced involuntarily in the articulation of given speech sounds."[42] " Involuntarily " with him obviously does not mean " inevitably," since he discusses errors of certain foreigners who fail to pronounce some of the glides properly.[43] The implication, then, is simply that by glides he means nondistinctive parts of some phonemic unit. Noël-Armfield conveys a similar implication when he says that, strictly, the term should " be used to express nothing more than a necessary intermediate sound between two regular speech-sounds [i.e. phonemes]."[44]

Sweet says that synthesis looks at a sound " as a momentary point in a stream of incessant change,"[45] but admits his inability to mark off the segments in this stream by admitting that for certain types " it is often difficult to know whether to write the glide or not."[46] Furthermore, when he starts dealing with sounds in speech he classifies practically everything as a glide: " Most consonants, as compared with vowels, have more or less the character of glides ";[47] flap con-

[39] Jones, §§ 3, 5.   [42] Passy, 89.   [45] Sweet, 44.
[40] Jones, § 219.   [43] Ibid.   [46] Sweet, 53.
[41] Jones, § 6 and n.   [44] Noël-Armfield, 61.   [47] Sweet, 64.

sonants are " pure glides " [48] as we have said; voiceless stops are, " acoustically speaking, pure glide-sounds "; [49] the aspiration of stops is a glide.[50]

If this aspiration glide is strong enough, it is said to become an " independent element." [51] Passy [52] likewise considers a reinforced glide to be an independent sound, and Jones speaks of such a sound as " practically a full independent [h] " [53] (this implies that when Jones previously stated of less strong aspiration that it was independent,[54] he meant something less than a separate segment). At this point phoneticians face a difficult problem if they wish to define a stop (or plosive consonant; Jones uses " stop " only for the closure [55]) as having to have three parts to be " complete." [56] When one of the factors is lacking, or one element is " independent," considerable adjustment has to be made in the segmentation.

Twaddell has a statement about a " phonetic fraction " which relates to the segments: " Corresponding to phonologically different forms are significantly different phonetic events. Each of these phonetic events is composed of phonetic fractions. These fractions are usually reckoned in terms of intervals during which the articulatory organs are substantially at rest, or are leaving such a position; intervals during which some articulatory organs are making a unidirectional movement; or intervals during which some articulatory organs are moving toward a position, maintain it substantially, and leave it. These fractions are, in short, what we call ' speech-sounds,' i.e. time-intervals of the actual utterance-events." [57] The principal difficulty with this as a working method for cutting out phonetic fractions is found in the overlapping criteria. How is one to tell whether a phenomenon wherein the organs move toward a position, maintain it, and leave it, composes one segment functioning as a whole; or one segment functioning as a fixed position; or three segments, with approaching, fixed, and releasing positions, and so on?

---

[48] *Ibid.* [51] Sweet, 58–59. [54] Jones, § 563.
[49] Sweet, 56. [52] Passy, 92. [55] Jones, § 562.
[50] Sweet, 56–57. [53] Jones, § 568.
[56] Jones, § 561; Noël-Armfield, 64; Passy, 71–72 (cf. 74, n. 1: " But of course for a complete [m] the mouth must be closed at the beginning and open at the end "); Ripman, *Elements of Phonetics*, 85 (in which the " momentary pause " can be left " out of account "!).
[57] Twaddell, 41–42.

If sounds with either moving or fixed positions can both be segments, some method must be devised to tell which criterion should be applied in particular situations. In lieu of that, phonemic structure rather than phonetic nature is certain to swing the balance one way or the other, as it did in the cases reviewed above.

Phonetic terminology and classification charts have been influenced by phonemics in regard to certain fluctuant segments, especially in the naming of certain groups as if they were single phonetic segments. Groups such as [tʃ] and [ts] have been called affricates; [nd], nasalized stops; [kw], labiovelars; [ph], aspirates; [ai], diphthongs. Why are there no unit names for groups such as [af], [fl], [rt], [to], and the like? Phonetically there is no explanation for this difference, since [gu] entails less change of articulation than [gw], [ba], the same as [ph], and so on. The explanation is perforce phonemic: in certain sound groups (at the fluctuant points) two segments frequently combine into single phonemes; as such they have acquired names. There is no objection to continuing such convenient terms or adding more, but they should be redefined strictly from a phonetic point of view. Bloch and Trager [58] are among the few writers who make this essential distinction by eliminating such groups from their phonetic classifications, but who provide at the same time convenient symbols for the use of the phonemicist.

Many short descriptions, and even some longer ones, of the phonetics of languages lack any attempt to define a speech sound.[59] In general, these are the same accounts which contain no discussion of nonspeech or marginal sounds.

As regards a continuum, the study in hand has two primary analytical aims: The first of these is to provide a means for cutting a continuum at any point, regardless of its relationship to other sounds or its natural segmentation, and to provide a terminology which will allow for the articulatory description of that sound in regard to certain specific major features of its production. This description makes no pretense at completeness, often ignoring finesse in fixing point of articulation and the like; the choice of factors for description is based

[58] Bloch and Trager, *Tables for a System of Phonetic Description* (Preliminary Ed.), 3.

[59] See Gairdner, *The Phonetics of Arabic;* Jones and Woo, *A Cantonese Phonetic Reader;* Karlgren, *A Mandarin Phonetic Reader (Archives d'Études Orientales,* Vol. 13) ; Stirling, *The Pronunciation of Spanish.*

primarily on strictural function (see pp. 56–65, 129–36, and 151–56). Such a piece of the continuum must include enough of the whole to form a perceptible impression on the ear. This is our *phonetic fraction* (see p. 116).

The second basic purpose with regard to the continuum is to provide a workable method for the delineation of natural phonetic segmentation. This has nothing to do with the articulatory description of the production of any particular sound except in so far as it becomes essential for the determining of the center or borders of a specific segmental unit. This segmental unit is to be determined entirely apart from phonemic function; if the influence of the latter creeps in unawares, as it almost certainly will at times because of phonemic prejudice from one's native language, to that extent the effort has failed. A corollary of this aim states that such a segmentation procedure is equally applicable to any and all languages, or to any stream of nonsense syllables. In so far as it may prove upon further testing to have come short of this goal, it must be revised.

The basic difficulty involved in segmentation (a difficulty due to individual variation in perceptual ability because of physiological limitations, phonemic background, or phonetic training) is taken care of in the procedure. The strategic fluctuants reach segmentation by the very same procedure as do all other sounds; the same criteria, for example, apply to [w], [p], [s], and [u]. One basic limitation remains to the segmentation technic here set forth: although it identifies the number of segments in a sequence (subject to the perceptual factor already mentioned), and points out the center of such segments, the borders cannot be strictly delineated. One cannot state the exact point where the division comes between segments, even though the centers are identifiable.

Once segmentation is complete, then segments of perceptually similar or identical sounds are grouped into *phonetic units,* which correspond directly with what in general usage is known as the " phone " except that phonetic units are more rigorously controlled as to size. The features selected for description can be consistently chosen on the basis of strictural function (rather than by phonemic assumptions or inconsistent factors), with the reservation that many smaller details — the exact point or degree of articulation, for example — which may be phonemically distinctive when the segment appears in speech, will inevitably be omitted from the phonetic description thus given. When the phonemicist points out to the phonetician certain other features in any phonetic unit which he wishes described, these can be added at will, within the limits of the articulatory procedure.

Since the number of segments in a particular continuum approaches the number of phonemes in that continuum, and the differences occur largely at well-known fluctuant points, an impressionistic phonetic record of a new language proves theoretically legitimate as well as practically valuable as a tool for the phonemicist in his analysis of the phonemic structure of that language. At the same time that it makes available a less prejudiced classification for the description of phonemes by an articulatory technic, it lays a better foundation for a study of the exact kinds of segments which can possibly be found to combine into single phonemes; Trubetzkoy presents material related to this possibility.[60] A segmental analysis should also give further validity to a nonphonemic study of speech such as the dialectologist produces.[61]

In this work a sound abstracted from speech, of indefinite extent but composed of no less than one segment and of no more segments than are known to be joined into single phonemes in some language, is a *speech sound*. The term is in contrast to related terms which have already been introduced (" phonetic fraction," " segment," " phonetic unit ").

By using the same criteria that were developed for the definition of the phonetic segment but applying them in a somewhat different manner, conditioned by the differing function of the moving parts of the vocal mechanism, we can arrive at an articulatory delineation of the *syllable*. This is quite similar to the description of the syllable given by Stetson in terms of chest pulses,[62] with three principal exceptions: (1) Stetson failed to allow for a perceptual factor and was

[60] Trubetzkoy, *Anleitung zu phonologischen Beschreibungen*, 13, (Édition du Cercle linguistique de Prague, Brno, 1935).

[61] For the necessity and validity of the nonphonemic approach in this connection see Bloch, Review of " Phonetic Transcriptions from ' American Speech ' " (edited by J. D. Zimmerman), *Lang.*, 16 (1940), 174–75; Kenyon, 36–37 (for both dialect geography and historical phonetic change).

[62] Stetson, 36: " The syllable is one in the sense that it consists essentially of a single chest pulse, usually made audible by a vowel, which may be started or stopped by a chest movement."

therefore forced to describe some groups of three sounds [63] (two non-syllabic consonants and a vowel) as containing two syllables, when the ear does not hear them so; his recordings of the chest pulses included some that were too weak to register audibly. He says, for example, of *pfeil*, and like words, that the second consonant sometimes becomes a " preliminary silent syllable followed by a voiced syllable." [64]   (2) He was confused by the spelling when he tried to describe consonant clusters. He says of certain of them, " languages differ in their handling of many of these groups. The German spells a group ' tsch,' which the French spells ' tch,' and the English ' ch.' " [65] (3) He shows that another criterion than that of chest pulses may have led him to his conclusion when he grants the possibility of sound groups such as [aia] or [ala] being made with single chest pulses but constituting two syllables; [66] in this case the oral movement would divide the syllables. He has no experimental evidence of the existence of this kind of syllable. Even if series of sounds of this type can be made with single chest pulses (and probably they can be, on the perceptual level at least), it appears preferable not to introduce a new criterion but to use one only — one based uniformly on strictural function (see below, p. 116). Introduction of a second type of articulatory criterion would probably undermine the consistency with which the first could be applied.

Other criteria which have been advanced for the syllable, such as relative loudness of the phonemes,[67] sonority,[68] prominence (made up of inherent sonority, length, stress, special intonation, or a combination of some of these),[69] and change in stress or pitch,[70] are not incompatible with an articulatory definition; these acoustic phenomena are the results of some articulatory movement, and might frequently be more convenient to use for description, if the two factors can be equated.

Some type of natural segmentation of sound sequences must be discoverable when even those who deny its existence use symbols

---

[63] Stetson (33) actually worked with sounds or segments of sound, and used symbols to represent different segments, even though he denied emphatically that they exist.

[64] Stetson, 124–25.

[65] Stetson, 121.

[66] Stetson, 58–59.

[67] See Bloomfield, 125.

[68] See Kenyon, 68–69.

[69] See Jones, §§ 209, 211, 215, 218.

[70] See Noël-Armfield, 51–52.

which assume this division. The smallest segmentation is into sounds. A larger segmentation which is related to it, but which functions differently in the continuum, is that of the syllable. The next chapter will attempt to show that within single sounds the productive movements do not all have the same function.

CHAPTER IV

STRICTURAL FUNCTION

IN THE production of sounds not all parts of the vocal mechanism act alike: neither all complete closures nor all partial ones have the same place in sound production, nor do the oral, nasal, and pharyngeal cavities. It is this difference in the action of various parts of the mechanism within the production of single sounds which is *strictural function*.

This type of internal function of parts of sound mechanisms contrasts sharply with an external type, *contextual function*, where sounds as complete units are related to one another in continuums as members of syllables or parts of a phonemic system.

Nowhere have I found any systematic discussion of such differences of internal function. In many respects the differences are ignored, and strictures serving dissimilar functions in a sound are treated on a level. Jespersen's analphabetic system,[1] for example, seems to give them all equal prominence without sufficient attempt at strictural differentiation.

Everywhere, however, functional differences are assumed. They enter into the warp and woof of every phonetic classification. In fact, no very significant articulatory phonetic (not phonemic) classification could possibly be made without some of these assumptions. In the next few pages I shall attempt to prove that such factors are present in sound production; to show that phonetic literature assumes or hints at many of them; and to demonstrate the need for a systematic presentation of such elements. Later a classification will be attempted (pp. 129–36), and a convenient descriptive order for these functional ranks postulated (pp. 151–56). It is this descriptive order which can give us a rational choice of basic items in describing a phonetic unit apart from phonemics.

[1] Jespersen, *The Articulations of Speech Sounds Represented by Means of Analphabetic Symbols.*

In sounds in which two mechanisms are operating at the same time (a combination of productive types; for details see pp. 94–103). a single stricture often has two different but simultaneous functions. The velar closure of a nasalized click offers an example. For the click part it is moving backward, drawing air into the mouth; of itself it produces no sound — the release of a closure farther forward does that (e.g. the release of the lips for a kiss). For the voiced nasalization it serves rather as a closed valve which prevents air escaping from the mouth and shunts the air out the open nasal passage, precisely as it does for an ordinary velar nasal which has no superimposed click. If, on the other hand, the nasal passage were closed, but the vocal cords were vibrating (for a " voiced click "), the velar closure would be functioning precisely as for a voiced velar stop [g], while at the same time in its other function it would be moving to empower the oral click.

A contrast of two functional types is mentioned by Westermann and Ward: the glottal closure is said to be secondary to a primary oral closure in ejectives.[2] Catford remarks that glottalic pressure stops (which are the same as Westermann and Ward's " ejectives " and the " glottalized stops " of this study) involve inevitably two releases, of which the outer is primary and the inner secondary; with velaric pressure or suction types the velaric release is secondary to primary outer release.[3]

The type thus labeled " secondary " has sometimes been called " inner closure."[4] This term does not clarify its functional peculiarity. On the one hand, it is not more inward than many other closures which do not enter the group (velar closure for [k] is not an " inner closure," nor is glottal closure for [ʔ]); on the other hand, when two closures are present, the innermost is not always an " inner closure " (as in double stops of [pk] type[5]), and one can actually have a functional " inner closure " which is outward in the mouth (see pp. 101–2). Function, not absolute or relative position, distinguishes

[2] Westermann and Ward, *Practical Phonetics for Students of African Languages*, 101.

[3] Catford, " On the Classification of Stop Consonants," *Le Maître Phonétique*, 3d Series, 65 (1939), 5.

[4] Bell, *Visible Speech* (Inaugural Ed.), 62; Catford, *op. cit.* in *Le Maître Phonétique*, 3d Series, 65 (1939), 2.

[5] See Noël-Armfield, *General Phonetics* [4], 119; Westermann and Ward, 107.

the type — the function of initiating the air stream (not of being a " suction stopper " [6]).

One of the most frequent and apparent differences of function is evidenced in the treatment of the opening leading to the nasal cavity. For convenience in this discussion the upper part of the soft palate facing the nasopharynx is the *velic* (so called in this discussion to distinguish it from the *velum*, which represents the lower side toward the mouth) ; the closure of the nasal passage is therefore a velic closure (in contrast to velar closure, when the tongue touches the soft palate).

Velic closure receives much less attention than closure of the lips or closure by the tongue, and the like. No phonetic treatment which I have seen includes in the definition of its technical term for the middle sound in [apa] any specific mention of velic closure; all of them take specific note of bilabial nature (i.e. " bilabial voiceless stop," never " velic bilabial voiceless stop "). In detailed description of stops a few books [7] meticulously include the velic closure; even these do not consistently mention the velic closure when a brief reference is made to particular stops after the full description has been given. More often the velic closure is assumed or receives a brief covering statement.[8] This difference in treatment between closures at velic and closures at oral points of articulation reflects a difference in function.

The oral closure, not the velic closure, is made to identify a particular stop. This applies regardless of whether or not the stop has oral approach or release, or both (as in [apa]), or whether it has velic approach or release, or both (as in [mbm]). If the velic closure were on a par with the oral closure, performing the same function, then the stops would have to be classified by either approach or release, since phonetically there would be no other way of determining whether the sound is a velic or an oral stop. Actually, phonemic usage of the sounds probably has a very great determining effect on the interpretation of the stop of [mbm] as a bilabial,[9] rather than a velic. This cannot be the entire explanation. An innate functional differ-

---

[6] Bell, 56.

[7] Jones, *An Outline of English Phonetics* [4], §§ 496, 511, 532 ; Kenyon, *American Pronunciation* [6], 40–44; Stirling, *The Pronunciation of Spanish*, 11.

[8] See, for example, Ripman, *Elements of Phonetics*, 1.

[9] For nasal and lateral release see Jones, §§ 499, 505, 513, 523, 535, 546, 586–90; Kenyon, 50.

ence must be reflected; otherwise why is not a velic stop a phoneme in any language? Why is it not given a place in phonetic alphabets apart from nasal release of an oral sound? Why is it so readily passed off as a convenient assumption? Why is it so difficult to teach students to remember the closure or to get a kinesthetic sense [10] of its presence? In fact, I have never seen a velic stop listed as a vocal sound separate from other stops except in Ripman, where it is called " velar " or " faucal." [11]

With continuants, the assumption of velic function (in contrast to explicit oral strictures) is more striking; the marked tendency is for authors to give no statement whatsoever of the velic position, simply assuming it to be closed, until suddenly in one section they note its lowering for nasalized sounds. Jones has three introductory chapters on vowels,[12] including a description of their cardinal values, in which no mention is made of velic position until, at the very end of the chapter, nasal vowels are discussed; [13] in later detailed descriptions it is mentioned for each vowel.[14] Passy leaves it entirely to assumption for both consonants and vowels,[15] except for nasals and nasalized types.[16]

The opening to the esophagus seems to be completely ignored. Yet in sounds with esophageal air (belches) it precisely parallels the glottis for pulmonic types. Its usual passive function is different from a lip closure or a velic closure when all three occur simultaneously in [p], yet it is closer to the latter than to the former.

There is general agreement among phoneticians [17] in treating cer-

[10] Differences in the sensitivity of the velic and tongue or lips can scarcely be the complete explanation, although they are undoubtedly influential in the determining of function, when the velic functions with extreme facility in the changing of oral to nasal sounds, and so on. Regardless of possible physiological explanation of function, the functional differences themselves are the important thing to note here.

[11] Ripman, 86.

[12] Jones, §§ 96–163.

[13] Jones, §§ 164–65.

[14] Jones, 63 n., §§ 255, 268, 277, 285, 298, 306, 316, 324, 335, 344, 395, 409, 422, 447, 456.

[15] Passy, *The Sounds of the French Language* [2], 60–62, 69.

[16] Passy, 62–64, 69.

[17] See Bloch and Trager, *Tables for a System of Phonetic Description* (Preliminary Ed.), 5; Gairdner, *The Phonetics of Arabic*, 20–21; Jones, § 533; Noël-Armfield, 96, 117–18; Sweet, *A Primer of Phonetics* [3], 37; Westermann and Ward, 107.

tain types of strictures as modifications of others; the modifications are " secondary " (and the others " primary," or " basic " sounds). The list includes labialization, palatalization, velarization, pharyngealization, and, in occasional accounts, a few others. Bloomfield has pointed out that this is not a phonemic distinction, nor one necessarily seen reflected in the systems of languages.[18] There seems to be some basic division here much deeper than mere convenience, however. One could protest against saying " alveolarly sibilantized labial " for " labialized [s] "; or " bilabially stopped palatal " for " palatalized [p]." The descriptive order appears to be chosen here on some real principle, not from fancy. Although this division is so widespread, and given representation in phonetic alphabets,[19] yet I have seen no concerted attempt to explain why certain strictures were considered basic and other strictures secondary, modifying them. The determining factor cannot be the point of articulation, since the lips are primary in [p] but secondary in labialized [s]; nor absolute amount of opening, since the same amount can be primary in [j] and secondary in palatalized [p]. There seems to be no effort to postulate all possible types of combination of two such secondary modifications for single sounds; Bloch and Trager mention one type, labiovelarization.[20]

Sounds in which two articulations are present, one regarded as primary (or basic) and the other secondary (or a modification), are seen even more significantly to be analyzed on the basis of some functional difference when they are contrasted with other types of sounds having two articulations which are not analyzed in this way. One of these is any oral sound with velic closure. That closure is not considered a " modification " (of, for example, the alveolar stricture in [s]), nor " basic " (which is reserved for the alveolar stricture in forming the sibilant). Another instance of two articulations neither of which comprises a modification is seen in double stops; Westermann and Ward point out this difference, in that neither of the closures is secondary or primary in respect to the other (in contrast to palatalized [p], where lips are primary).[21] In the various types of clicks and similar sounds the " inner closure " would enter neither

[18] Bloomfield, *Language*, 109.

[19] See Heepe, *Lautzeichen und ihre Anwendung in verschiedenen Sprachgebieten*, and, more recently, Bloch and Trager.

[20] Bloch and Trager, 7.

[21] Westermann and Ward, 107.

the " primary " nor " secondary " groups; compare a labialized click [t], where the lips form a modification, the tongue tip a primary closure, and the velar closure is different from either one.

In spite of the fact that lip rounding of vowels is sometimes said to be secondary,[22] this cannot be equated with function of labialization of consonants. One can scarcely say that [u] is a " labialized basic back vowel," since [u] seems to have basic character of its own, fully as much as does an unrounded high back vowel; [u] does not sound like an unrounded back vowel with something extraneous added, but sounds, rather, like a new entity. A functional difference is involved in this distinction.

Oral and nasal cavities are treated in entirely different ways; functionally the nasal cavity is treated as secondary to the oral one. This is not always admitted. Bloch and Trager state that the oral–nasal division is considered basic,[23] but later under resonance types, instead of paralleling oral with nasal, they parallel oral with nasalization; that is, a combination of oral plus nasal, in which the latter takes a secondary, modifying, place.[24]

Were oral and nasal cavities to be treated as functionally equal, " oral vowels " would parallel " nasal vowels " (that is, [m], [n], not nasalized vowels); [a] would parallel [ŋ] (since for [a] the velic closes the back of the nasal cavity, whereas for [ŋ] the tongue closes the back of the oral cavity); [m] would parallel nasalized [a] with velic open but nostrils pinched closed (since for [m] the front of the oral cavity is closed but the remainder is used for resonance, whereas for [a] the velic's being open would allow the nasal cavity to be used for resonance while it was closed at the front end by the nostrils); [χ] would parallel a velic fricative (since [χ] has closure at the back of the nasal cavity but friction at the back of the oral one, while a velic fricative has back oral closure plus back nasal friction). Furthermore, if both cavities were wide open, a new type of sound would be produced, an " oral-nasal," in which neither cavity would predominate and neither would be secondary; actually this type of sound is called a nasalized vowel — never an " oralized nasal " — showing that the nasal cavity is considered secondary. The two parallel cav-

[22] See Gairdner, 34; Noël-Armfield, chart facing 180; cf. also Bloomfield, 105.
[23] Bloch and Trager, 2.
[24] Bloch and Trager, 7.

ities could be diagrammed in a kind of F form, in which the lower cavity can be closed at any point by lips or tongue; but the upper can be closed only at the back by the velic (or at the front, by the fingers pinching the nostrils).

To complicate the picture further, Bloch and Trager appear to call the nasals " nasal stops." [25] Since it is obvious that such sounds are not stops, but continuants, one must assume either that the terminology is chosen because of phonemic usage of the sounds as consonants, in a way similar to stops, or that the points of articulation of the oral closure in each case may be the same. Neither of these reasons would lead to such an association of stops and nasals if the oral and nasal division were treated as fundamental, and (therefore) if free nasal egress of air with oral closure were paralleled with free oral egress with nasal closure.

One sees, then, that resonance of the nasal cavity has been treated as secondary to resonance of the oral cavity. Nevertheless, this type of modification cannot be equated with the type which is caused simply by adding another oral stricture, as Bloch and Trager very definitely show in their outline; [26] that is, modification by nasalization functions differently from modification by strictures such as labialization.

That articulatory movements and sounds (apart from voice) in the pharynx have been given little study, and have little place in phonemic systems, we have already mentioned.[27] It may be that phonemic systems use such items so infrequently because they are in some way subordinate as regards structural function. One can give further evidence of the subordinate nature of all sounds below the oral cavity, as far as speech is concerned. In speaking, it appears that absolutely nothing a person can do, with the exception of cutting off sound by glottal or pharyngeal stops, changes the sequence of consonant and vowel phonemic types. Why does a vowel retain similar basic characteristics when whispered (some writers urge whispering of sounds for analysis since their character is then more clearly recognized [28]) as when voiceless or voiced(?) murmured(?) in falsetto(?) with pharyngeal or faucal constriction(?) Presumably it

[25] The nasal stops ("nasalized" is also implied) mentioned in (2) are apparently to be identified with the nasals on chart 5 (see also Ripman, 13).

[26] Bloch and Trager, 7.

[27] See p. 8.

[28] See Gairdner, 32; Sweet, 23.

indicates a difference in function between oral strictures and those of the pharyngeal cavity. Even those sounds which are phonemic norms, produced in the pharynx, tend to be misunderstood (see Sweet and Passy for pharyngeal spirants labeled bronchial ones [29]). Voicing is treated entirely differently from any other modification, with a function distinct from that of labialization and the like. With but few exceptions,[30] voicing is classified as causing one of the basic consonant divisions,[31] but, in contrast, not as causing vowel divisions.[32]

Whereas contact, or even narrowing, at the center of an air passage is always considered important (e.g. for making a fricative consonant closure, or producing contact for a lateral), the very same, or even far greater, contact at the side of the air passage (e.g. for [i] or [s] or rounded lips) goes unclassified or even unnoted except that such contact is used with palatograms [33] for determining by implication the size and height of the opening, and so on; the contact itself is either ignored as being unimportant, or else it is tacitly assumed that such contact naturally follows if one describes a certain opening. Nevertheless, the contrast of side contact with central contact, and the contrast of contact which partly closes an opening with contact which completely closes an opening, represent marked functional differences which should be classified more expressly. If Kenyon uses contact at the center of the tongue (as distinct from a side opening) to prove [1] a consonant,[34] why has not the same argument been used with equal legitimacy to prove that the side contact on [i], which produces the narrowing he mentions,[35] makes it also a consonant (instead of an appeal being made to resonance criteria to show this)? Only tacitly assumed functional differences in the types of contact can explain such a divergence of treatment.

Should all assumptions of differences of strictural function be eliminated from phonetic discussion, articulatory classification would be

[29] See p. 8, n. 41, for references.

[30] Sweet's classification of voiced consonants is obscure because he relates them to vowels (31).

[31] See Jones, § 173; Kenyon, 46; Noël-Armfield, 28; Passy, 68; Sweet, 31, 41.

[32] Cf. p. 5, n. 1; also Chapter V, " Classification Criteria," p. 72.

[33] See Jones, §§ 79–81, figs. 37, 39, and so on; Kenyon, 60; Noël-Armfield, 142–47.

[34] Kenyon, 58–59.

[35] Kenyon, 59.

vastly different and drastically hampered. Two of the criteria remaining would be the degree of closure and the number of strictures of each such degree. If, for example, two degrees of closure were used, complete closure and partial closure, a study by number of strictures only would fail to separate the following obviously different types:

Nasals and [a] and glottal stop; all have one complete closure (velic, oral, glottal, respectively);

Egressive-click fricatives and oral pulmonic fricatives; each has one complete closure (velar, velic) and one partial one;

Pulmonic stops (except [?]) and (oral) click stops; both have two closures (velic and oral, velar and front oral); in a similar way, modified pulmonic stops (modified by labialization, and so on) and modified click stops could not be separated (each has a single partial stricture added to its basic type);

Glottalized stops and double pulmonic stops; both have three full closures (glottal, velic, front oral; velic and two oral);

Compressive and rarefaction types of stops of fricatives, in any one mechanism (since the number of strictures, degrees, and places of closure are all the same).

Even in this list at least one functional assumption crept in, the ignoring of esophageal closure. Were this factor included, it would change the grouping and obscure relationships further by adding another closure to pulmonic and glottalized types, but not to glottal stop or to (oral) clicks. The samples were chosen also to prevent the entrance of the complicating factor of side contact in vowels and the like. Nonspeech sounds would show other parallels in addition to these, but the basis has not yet been laid for discussing them.

An articulatory classification to be workable must postulate differences of function or rank in various types of closures, narrowings, and partial contacts, as well as functional differences between the cavities themselves.

Once different ranks are classified, the description of any phonetic unit may contain items from each of certain ranks, if they cause changes of sound above the perceptual threshold for the particular observer. In this way, after the phonetician has isolated his own units without phonemic aid, he can also give a rough articulatory description of them without particular phonemic admixture. The details that he cannot describe he must leave subsumed under these rough articulatory labels as a partial superimposing of imitation-label material. If he is capable of describing certain differences which do not occur within his chosen descriptive patterns, he must wait for the phonemicist (or some phonetic project such as a linguistic atlas) to call attention to the need for a discussion of them. This to some extent would relieve the phonetician of the onus of describing without plan anything and everything he can hear, by setting up a definite program for the description of certain basic phonomena of strictural function.

CHAPTER V

CLASSIFICATION CRITERIA

THE most basic,[1] characteristic, and universal division made in phonetic classification is that of consonant and vowel. Its delineation is one of the least satisfactory — a difficulty passed on to the instrumentalist.[2] Frequently for descriptions of single languages the division is assumed, with no attempt to define it.[3] The distinction is often presented as if it were clear-cut, with every sound belonging to one or the other of the groups. Jones, for example, says, " Every speech-sound belongs to one or other of the two main classes known as Vowels and Consonants."[4] Later, however, various sounds are mentioned by him which have to be discussed separately under different rules, or with various kinds of reservation, because they do not neatly catalog themselves.[5] Occasionally, in contrast to this, a writer frankly admits that his definition either of vowels or of consonants is unsatisfactory.[6]

The most important reason for the difficulty at the border line between consonants and vowels is that many criteria, and criteria of conflicting status, are used. When these various criteria are strictly applied, each of them draws the boundary at a different place; the groups determined by the several criteria do not coincide. In this predicament it is left to the " predominating " feature or features to decide which criterion shall classify particular sounds.[7] Such an

[1] See Bloch and Trager, *Tables for a System of Phonetic Description* (Preliminary Ed.), 2.

[2] Cf. Fletcher, *Speech and Hearing*, 7.

[3] See, for example, Forchhammer, *How to Learn Danish*[4]; Ward, *An Introduction to the Ibo Language*. See also *The Principles of the International Phonetic Association*, Supplement to *Le Maître Phonétique*.

[4] Jones, *An Outline of English Phonetics*[4], § 96.

[5] See Jones, 46, n. 5, §§ 183, 227, 231, 793, 799.

[6] See Noël-Armfield, *General Phonetics*[4], 9 n.; Westermann and Ward, *Practical Phonetics for Students of African Languages*, 20 n.

[7] See Kenyon, *American Pronunciation*[6], 57; Passy, *The Sounds of the French Language*[2], 4–5.

expedient disguises the real problem without solving it, since the decision as to which factor is predominating is arrived at by still other criteria, and, to make the matter worse, these often are not set forth clearly, if they are stated at all. Articulatory, acoustic, and contextual criteria are three of the basic types used to determine whether sounds are consonants or vowels; they will be treated below in this order.

Obstruction of the air stream at times constitutes one articulatory criterion for consonants.[8] This by itself is insufficient. With stops, the obstruction is complete, and no question arises about their consonantal nature, but continuants cause a problem, since some of them are classed as fricatives (e.g. [s]), while others are regarded as vowels, even though both types have partial obstructions. The criterion which determines whether a partial obstruction constitutes a consonant-causing obstruction (rather than a vocalic lack of obstruction) is not wholly articulatory.[9] What does constitute obstruction of the kind to make consonants? If contact at the sides of the tongue, or small height of opening (so that a small hole is left for air to escape), is such, then [i] would be a consonant, since Kenyon notes that it may have more tongue contact than [1].[10] There seems to be no articulatory measuring rod for degree of constriction or obstruction which marks the consonant–vowel border. Even a velic closure in oral vowels keeps the air stream from escaping by the nose, and so a pure obstruction criterion which ignored rank of stricture (see above, pp. 61–62) would label oral vowels as consonants.

Narrowing[11] as a criterion fares precisely as does contact;[12] no articulatory measure for degree of contact or narrowing is provided to show the point at which a vowel becomes a consonant. If one starts

<hr />

[8] See Bloomfield, *Language*, 102; Jones, §§ 97, 99; Nicholson, *A Practical Introduction to French Phonetics*, 42; Noël-Armfield, 9; Ripman, *Elements of Phonetics*, 10, 12; Soames, *Introduction to English, French and German Phonetics*[3], 33; Stirling, *The Pronunciation of Spanish*, 6; Sweet, *A Primer of Phonetics*[3], 22, 31; Viëtor, *German Pronunciation*[5], 36; Westermann and Ward, 19–20.

[9] See acoustic types (pp. 70–72) for criterion of audible friction.

[10] Kenyon, 60.

[11] See Jones, § 97; Kenyon, 57–59; Nicholson, 42; Ripman, 12; Soames, 33; Sweet, 31; Viëtor, 36. See also Jespersen (*The Articulations of Speech Sounds Represented by Means of Analphabetic Symbols*) for degrees of opening.

[12] See Bloomfield, 102; Kenyon, 57–59.

with a little narrowing, caused in turn by slight contact, and gradually increases contact to produce further narrowing, oral sounds will generally have begun as vowels and ended as consonants, with no articulatory marking [13] of the transition.

One clear articulatory essential for a vowel is that at least part of the air must be coming out of the mouth, although part may also be escaping through the nose.[14] This eliminates stops and nasals from vocalic classification, but it does not separate oral consonants from oral vowels.

Jones and Kenyon use movement as a criterion for certain consonants (glides, [j], [w]) in contrast to vowels, which are said to have fixed, or relatively fixed, position; [15] but Jones also uses movement as a criterion for certain types of vowels (diphthongs [16]). The criterion is vitiated when he shows variants of both the glides and the diphthongs, written with the same letters (or the same letters plus a length sign), which are not quick glides but have at least part of the sound relatively fixed.[17] He states that the two are difficult to distinguish in certain combinations [18] and fails to set forth the method for determining which is which.[19] Further, for the less prominent part of a diphthong he uses the term "consonantal vowel," which he states is not quite accurate, without giving reasons,[20] though perhaps he objects to suggesting that a vowel has consonant characteristics. To say the least, these difficulties demonstrate that the line of demarcation between vowel and consonant is not too readily drawn,[21] and that Jones's criteria are not too easily applied. One might reason that no positions are fixed, but all are fluid, and therefore that no movement criterion is valid; the movement, however, might in certain instances be below the perceptual level or near it, and

[13] Cf. pp. 138–39.

[14] See Bloomfield, 102; Jones, §§ 97, 99; Passy, 56; Westermann and Ward, 19–20.

[15] Jones, §§ 102, 800, 813; Kenyon, 59, 152, 155, 233.

[16] Jones, § 219. Presumably Jones considers diphthongs vowels, if every sound is either consonant or vowel (§ 96).

[17] Jones, §§ 227, 799.

[18] Jones, 58, n. 11, § 226.

[19] Presumably the primary criterion is contextual function, to be discussed below, pp. 73–77.

[20] Jones, § 231.

[21] As is well known. Cf. Soames, 33.

hence give rise to contrast between perceptual movement and perceptual lack of movement. One therefore could make no objection on this particular basis to movement as a criterion.

Certain other factors (speed, force, voicing) with articulatory relationships are more conveniently discussed under contextual criteria. These will be given attention below (see pp. 73–77).

Two acoustic criteria of importance are used in separating vowels and consonants. The vowels are considered to be the sounds which are naturally more sonorous and resonant than the consonants.[22] At this point the sonority with which we are concerned is that which might be applied as a criterion to sounds in isolation. Sonority which is studied as relatively greater for one sound than for another in a particular context is a separate matter (see below, pp. 70–71). The sonority that classes a sound as a vowel or consonant regardless of its surroundings is an acoustic (not a contextual) criterion.

Strangely enough, phoneticians seem usually to establish their consonant–vowel groupings by some such criterion in conjunction with contextual types, and then attempt to define or defend such divisions by mechanical, articulatory technics, ignoring the very factors which originally caused the postulation of the division. Jones (§ 97), for example, first defines a vowel as being " a voiced sound in forming which the air issues in a continuous stream through the pharynx and mouth, there being no obstruction and no narrowing such as would cause friction." Then later he elucidates his reason for choosing such a delineation: "It so happens that the sounds defined as vowels in § 97 are noticeably more sonorous than any other speech-sounds (when pronounced in a normal manner); and that is the reason why these sounds are considered to form one of the two fundamental classes." [23]

This statement Jones modifies by an important footnote in which he admits that cardinal [i] is apparently less sonorous than some other speech sounds. Kenyon also shows that certain sonants (e.g. [l] sounds) are very resonant, almost enough so to come under definitions of vocalic sonority; [24] he is forced to use other criteria (tone quality and front contact) to prevent that classification. Passy likewise sees

[22] See Kenyon, 57; Westermann and Ward, 89, 110.
[23] Jones, § 100.
[24] Kenyon, 60.

that strict application of such criteria would tend to the classification of sonants as vowels, but exclaims that linguistic instinct protests against the idea.[25] Such factors demonstrate conclusively that natural sonority is not at all the complete reason for basic vowel–consonant classification; linguistic instinct is formed primarily by contextual function. Nevertheless, natural sonority seems to have a very large influence on consonant–vowel delineation as one important factor determining contextual function itself. Nonsyllabic vowels of [a] or [e] type and the like [26] (in diphthongs) give one of the strongest evidences of natural sonority as a criterion for their vocalic classification, since at that point contextual prominence is not so marked.

The second main acoustic criterion is friction, and is used to some extent by practically all writers on the subject.[27] Sounds wherein some obstruction causes audible friction are thereby considered to be consonants. Friction in this way proves to be a test of the degree of obstruction for vowel and consonant differentiation. Of itself, an articulatory technic cannot establish this boundary since, as we have already shown (p. 67), obstruction passes from vowel type to consonant type by imperceptible degrees, while differences of strictural function also affect the result. At this point auditory acoustic technic supplements the articulatory one by providing a helpful criterion.

Actually, however, the test is not consistently applied. For sounds such as [f] and [s] there is no doubt; they are obviously consonants. But certain sounds classified as vowels (close types) may actually contain audible friction,[28] while, on the other hand, many sounds without audible friction (voiced sonants) [29] are nevertheless considered to be consonants. Various writers mention this difficulty.[30]

Even with friction and sonority as criteria, the border line between consonants and vowels is uncertain, hazy, and wavering. Friction,

[25] Passy, *Petite phonétique comparée* [3], 14.

[26] See Jones, §§ 225, 423, 466.

[27] See Bloomfield, 102; Jones, 31, n. 5–6, §§ 97, 99, 811; Nicholson, 42; Noël-Armfield, 8, 9; Passy, *Phonétique*, 108; *Sounds*, 67, 86 (and noise, 68); Soames, 42; Sweet, 13, 22; Westermann and Ward, 19.

[28] See Jones and Woo, *A Cantonese Phonetic Reader*, xii; Karlgren, *A Mandarin Phonetic Reader* (*Archives d'Études Orientales*, Vol. 13), 6–7; Noël-Armfield, 9 n.; Passy, *Sounds*, 15; Sweet, 22.

[29] See Jones, 24 n., 183, 749, 796; Kenyon, 48. But see Noël-Armfield, 9 n., and Passy, *Sounds*, 70, 73, who hear slight friction in such sounds.

[30] See Noël-Armfield, 9 n.; Westermann and Ward, 20 n.

designed to measure the amount of obstruction, in turn needs something to measure its degree of noise, since it shades from no perceptible noise to strong amounts,[31] from zero audible friction in voiced open vowels and sonants to slight friction in certain close vowels and sonants and to considerable amounts in fricatives. The measuring rod actually used generally proves to be contextual function.

One of the marked weaknesses in current usage of friction as a criterion for consonant–vowel differentiation lies in the failure to distinguish satisfactorily between two types of friction which function very differently and have different origins, even though the border lines are not sharp between them. Generally speaking, one type retains its audibility when voiced (e.g. for sibilants); the other is a weak fricative and audible only when sounds are voiceless [32] (e.g. most vowels, certain sonants). The first type results from stricture at a single *local* point; the second is due to *cavity friction,* that is, voiceless resonance of a chamber as a whole [33] caused by air going through it as through an open tube. Friction of either type may occur in cavities of different rank and function. To lump together as fricatives all sounds derived in these two ways, or to classify all of them immediately as consonants, because of friction, regardless of the type of friction or the rank of the cavity in which it occurs, invites difficulty and inconsistency in the separation of vowels and consonants.

By working with these two degrees of friction and combining them at the same time with a classification of strictural function which subordinates pharyngeal and glottal activity to oral types (see pp. 129–33), one can arrive at a significant statement concerning the phonetic patterning of [h], in relation to voiceless vowels, and whispers, and " voiced [h]." [34] Both voiceless and voiced vowels have cavity friction; as with other types of cavity friction, the first tend to be audible and the second inaudible. If to each type one adds local

---

[31] Cf. Bloomfield, 97.

[32] See Jones, § 820, for one illustration of local and cavity friction (voiceless fricative [j] and voiceless semivowel [j]), which are hard to tell apart; the high tongue position for the cavity almost localizes the friction, causing the difficulty.

[33] See Kenyon, 57.

[34] Cf. Jespersen, *Lehrbuch der Phonetik* [4], 91–93; Jones, § 779; Kenyon, in Webster, § 44 (10); Noël-Armfield, 109–12; Sweet, 55; Westermann and Ward, 86.

glottal friction, the first gives whispered vowels [35] and the second vocalic timbres of " voiced [h]," creating the proportion, voiceless vowel (i.e. [h]) : whispered vowel :: voiced vowel : " voiced [h]." The letters [h] and [ɦ] would simply be convenient symbols representing any vocalic mouth position with the requisite inner modifications. That [h] may be used to function in the system of a particular language in a way similar, for example, to [p], [n], or [s] (rather than [a] or [u]) is a factor of contextual function which should not affect the description of the sound in a classification built upon characteristics of the method of production. Contextual influence upon the description of [h] will be pointed out a bit later (pp. 76–77).

Presumably the criterion of sonority is partly responsible for the entrance of voicing into vowel definitions.[36] Conversely, the criterion of friction has been partly responsible for the elimination of voiceless or whispered vowels [37] from those definitions (contextual function appears to have been the cause of their retention as " vowels " of abnormal type).

In languages the nasals seem to have no voiced type with local (velic) friction, but only a type with cavity friction. The same is true of the voiceless type; hence the friction is very soft.[38] Laterals usually, but not always, have inaudible cavity friction when voiced, but upon becoming voiceless narrow the opening sufficiently to get local friction [39] (so producing the difference in strength of friction between voiceless [n] and [l] mentioned by Bloomfield [40]). Voiced frictionless sonants may be said to be similar to vowels in resonance, but when the sonants are voiceless their cavity (or local) friction seems to have prevented this comparison; [41] actually it should not do so, since the vowels when voiceless also have cavity friction.

If both articulatory and acoustic criteria are to be used to distinguish consonants from vowels, a descriptive order is needed for

[35] For structural function in the closure of the vocal cords and opening of the whisper glottis see p. 136.

[36] See p. 5, n. 1.

[37] Cf. Jones, §§ 776–77; Kenyon, 38; Noël-Armfield, 8 n.; Westermann and Ward, 85; Ripman, 21, 59.

[38] Cf. Bloomfield, 96; Noël-Armfield, 9, n. 1; Sweet, 31.

[39] Cf. Bloomfield, 102.

[40] Bloomfield, 96–97.

[41] See Jones, 24, n. 3; Kenyon, 60; Noël-Armfield, 9, n. 1; Sweet, 31; cf. Bloomfield, 102.

their application. A certain criterion should always be applied first, another second, and so on, regardless of where the procedure leads; it cannot give exactly the same results as are now obtained. There is no objection to supplementing articulatory criteria with auditory acoustic aids if they can be controlled; in fact, we have suggested above (pp. 71–72) an extension of types of friction criteria. However, the application of these criteria must be in strict order, or overlapping groups will be obtained; consistent results necessitate consistent procedure.

Contextual function is the third major type of criterion which phoneticians have used for distinguishing vowels from consonants. Where one sound is affected in any way in its classification because of its relationship to neighboring sounds or to a system, contextual function has caused the change, instead of its position having been determined by its own absolute articulatory or acoustic nature. Contextual function of segments is of two kinds: (1) function in a larger phonetic unit, the syllable, or (2) function in a linguistic system as a phoneme with pattern relationships.

Stetson states that the decision whether a sound is a consonant or a vowel depends upon " what it does in the syllable." [42] If he were consistent in the application of this criterion, every syllabic would be a vowel, and every nonsyllabic a consonant. This shows contextual function of the type which is phonetic because of the relationship of the sound to a phonetic unit, the syllable.

Jones uses contextual function in vowel–consonant classification in many different ways. One of these has to do with relative force. Sounds which would be vowels in isolation he classes in one place as consonants because they are weaker than certain others in the immediate context: " The palatal and velar frictionless continuants have the organic positions of close vowels. In fact they are vowels, but they are uttered with very little breath force as compared with the normally pronounced vowels which adjoin them in connected speech. These frictionless continuants are to be considered as consonants on account of their consequent lack of prominence as compared with the adjoining vowels." [43]

The same relative (contextual) criterion of force is used in con-

[42] Stetson, " Motor Phonetics . . . ," *Arch. Néer. Phon. Expér.*, 3 (1928), 20.
[43] Jones, 46, n. 5.

junction with other criteria when Jones states that glides (or even sounds in the same phoneme but not gliding [44]) are consonants rather than vowels; the decisive factor is their " lack of stress as compared with the succeeding vowel." [45]

A similar situation is seen in regard to quantity. The shortness or rapidity of a sound relative to others is used by Jones and Kenyon as one criterion for the consonantal nature of glides.[46]

Voegelin mentions that Shawnee exhibits the usual vowel–consonant distinction " on distributional as well as on phonetic grounds." [47] That distribution feature which Voegelin has here pointed out as a phonemicist is probably the most influential of all criteria for actually determining the border lines at which particular phoneticians separate consonants from vowels. Although many articulatory or acoustic criteria may be mentioned by an author, somehow the resultant groupings always reflect the phonemic division as seen in permitted groupings of phonemes, sequences of syllabics, and the like. This is the reason that the articulatory and acoustic criteria already discussed have not been consistently applied, since they were not the deciding factors; authors have simply attempted to give an articulatory rationalization of the consonant–vowel division after it had been reached (consciously or unconsciously) on contextual grounds.

Phoneticians of course want practical results. Yet " practical " divisions, like " linguistic instinct," tend to reflect linguistic usage, which in turn inevitably means contextual function. Kenyon demonstrates the relationship between the " practical " criterion and the distributional one: " Vowels and consonants have many features in common. It is the predominating features that are significant for each class by itself. These predominating features determine the practical use of the vowel and consonant sounds in actual speech." [48] " Walker (1791) pointed out that the sounds [w] and [j] were treated popularly as consonants in actual unconscious speech by the use of the indefinite article [ə] ([ə wɔk, ə jok]). Likewise today the definite article [ðə] and the preposition [tə] are used ([ðə wɔk, ðə jok, tə wɔɚ, tə juɚ·əp]) as before other words beginning with consonants.

---

[44] Jones, § 799.
[45] Jones, §§ 102, 800.
[46] Jones, §§ 102, 800; Kenyon, 155.
[47] Voegelin, " Shawnee Phonemes," *Lang.*, 11 (1935), 23–37.
[48] Kenyon, 57; cf. p. 233.

But [ən], [ðɪ], and [tʊ] are used before [u], [i], and [ʒ] ([ən uzɪŋ sprɪŋ, ðɪ ist, tʊ ʒdʒ], etc.)."⁴⁹

Instead of the predominating features determining use in speech, use in speech has determined Kenyon's choice of "predominating features." In appealing to popular use he appeals to his most basic (but assumed) criterion, contextual function. The sandhi of addition of [n] in the indefinite article before vowels merely shows that [w] and [j] are in the same distributional group with [p], [s], and so on; it proves nothing as to the innate articulatory movements producing the sound, or as to the acoustic result. When, on the one hand, Kenyon's acoustic and articulatory criteria are not consistently applied, but, on the other, his divisions correspond fairly closely to phonemic ones, the conclusion is inescapable that his basic criteria have been phonemic assumptions. Presumably some such factor explains his surprising conclusion that [w], [j], and [r] when in certain prevocalic positions are consonants, but when final in [ai], [aw], and [aɚ] are " nonsyllabic vowels, both in function and organic nature."⁵⁰ Change in phonemic usage should not change phonetic description if the absolute nature of the sound is considered to be unchanged.

If a syllabic is established acoustically by relative loudness⁵¹ or prominence⁵² it cannot be any innate natural sonority which always forces certain sounds to be syllabic, or else there could never be any variation between a sound which, in the same phonetic context, is sometimes syllabic and sometimes not, like English sonants [l], [r], [m], and [n], or like nonsyllabic vowels. The syllabic nature of any particular utterance of a sound is produced by a type of syllabic function which in turn is a type of contextual function even though this function is conditioned by articulatory movements.

When Jones says that " It is as a consequence of this principle of relative prominence that certain short vowel-glides must be regarded as consonants,"⁵³ we are immediately aware that he is using contextual function as his criterion. Since we have already mentioned his use of two other contextual factors (relative force and relative duration) but of only one articulatory one (movement — and this is

⁴⁹ Kenyon, 60.
⁵⁰ Kenyon, 234.
⁵¹ See Bloomfield, 125.
⁵² See Jones, §§ 209, 211, 215, 218; Noël-Armfield, 51.
⁵³ Jones, § 102.

not consistently applied) it becomes obvious that for Jones, as well as for Kenyon, glides are consonants, not because of their basic articulatory or acoustic structure, but simply because of function in a phonetic or phonemic context.

Syllabic contextual function is reflected in phonetic alphabets. Sounds which are described by the same procedure but which are used differently in phonemic systems as syllabics in contrast to nonsyllabics are given different symbols,[54] and at times are given names such as " semivowel " and the like. This is occasionally an evidence of indecision on the part of the authors as to whether certain sounds should be considered consonants or vowels (or some type halfway between, in spite of a desired sharp division between vowels and consonants [55]) when contextual criteria point in one direction but acoustic and articulatory features of the segments point in another.

In addition to the factors of sonority, friction (see p. 72), and speech normality (see pp. 5–6), which have determined the exclusion of voiceless vowels from vowel definition, contextual factors have contributed to that result. In spite of the fact that Jones allows only for voiced types in his vowel definition, he admits in various places that [h] sounds " are simply vowels pronounced with breath instead of voice " [56]; the [h] sounds could in " a very narrow transcription " be written with voiceless vowel symbols, but such a mode of representation would be " both inconvenient and unnecessary." [57] The reason it is unnecessary is that the different voiceless vowels constitute a single phoneme in English, which would not be at all true if thev were in phonemic contrast.

The distributional criterion is seen in Kenyon, where [h] is said to occur only before " sounds with unobstructed outflow of breath " [58]; this is an item of English phonemic distribution having no essential relationship to [h] types as acoustic phenomena since they can also be pronounced in isolation or in other phonetic contexts. Kenyon objects to considering any [h] a voiceless vowel; [59] the phonemicist who must study languages yet unreduced to writing knows, however,

[54] See Bloch and Trager, 2.
[55] See Noël-Armfield, 9, n. 1.
[56] Jones, §§ 782, 777, 783, p. 186, n. 43.
[57] Jones, 186, n. 43; § 777.
[58] Kenyon, 138.
[59] Kenyon, in Webster, § 44 (10).

that he cannot tell whether a certain sound is an " h " or a " voiceless vowel " until he can classify its distributions and contrasts to see how it patterns with other consonants or vowels.

Jespersen states that " to be conceived as an [h] the voiceless vowel must be pronounced immediately before or behind a voiced vowel." [60] This represents a still different setup for distributional determination of consonant and vowel.

The question needs to be raised as to what are the aims of phonetic description. Are they to show the acoustic or articulatory characteristics of sounds, or are they rather to show interrelationships of the sounds of systems? Regardless of which the phonetician feels is his task, or whether he undertakes both, the two aims must be kept strictly apart. The phonemicist, dealing with the second, has come to see that from the point of view of the description of the functional structure of a system the particular phonetic value of a sound is not always especially pertinent to its place in the system; [61] the essential element is a group of acoustic symbols in certain interrelationships.

The phonetician has not yet realized that for describing the nature of a sound its phonemic relationship to other sounds and its relative value, rather than its absolute type, are in turn not pertinent to his description of the sounds themselves. In fact, to the very extent that the phonetician makes his classification dependent upon contextually relative features, he has made himself incapable of describing the sounds as units themselves. If the single sounds of a continuum cannot be described without reference to each other, then the continuum can be described only as a whole, not in parts; but if its parts cannot be described first, how can it be described as a whole?

A phonetic system should be able, within the limits of the accuracy and finesse of its articulatory, acoustic, or imitation-label procedures, to describe any sound in isolation, or in nonsense syllables, or as cut from a continuum of speech, without the necessity of referring to other sounds in the context to find criteria for its classification. A phonetic science should be able to define and describe its own units by its own data; if it cannot, how can it later describe for the phonemicist the speech system which the latter has presented? If the

[60] Jespersen, *Articulations*, 71.
[61] Cf. Bloomfield, " Menomini Morphophonemics," *Études phonologiques dédiées à la mémoire de M. le prince N. S. Trubetzkoy (Travaux du Cercle linguistique de Prague*, Vol. 8), 107, n. 1.

phonetician first delimits supposed articulatory classes by phonemic features, how can he then describe the phonemes with articulatory methods? Any such attempt presents a vicious circle of phonemics to phonetics to phonemics, with the phonetician starting at phonemics. A sound is the same sound wherever it occurs — but for the phonetician who uses essentially variable phonemic criteria to describe that sound, it may become a chameleon and change its color in different languages or even at different points in the same language.

In this study I attempt to draw up a phonetic scheme in which any sound can be described without reference to contextual function of the phonemic kind (i.e. sounds in speech). The invention of a considerable amount of new terminology has been essential, in spite of the fact that many current terms have been retained after redefinition.

Vocoid and *contoid* groups are strictly delineated by the articulatory and acoustic nature of sounds, without reference to phonemic contextual function. The terms approximate current groupings of vowel and consonant in some of their major phonetic characteristics.

Vowels and *consonants* are then categories of sounds, not as determined by their own phonetic nature, but according to their grouping in specific syllable contextual functions. This definition is flexible, awaiting elaboration or phonemic modification for each particular language after phonemic contextual data for the language have been assembled.

I have found just one work (Bloomfield) which makes the division between a general phonetic articulatory definition of vowel and consonant, and a phonemic definition for particular languages; unfortunately, this excellent lead has not been followed by subsequent phonetic writers. Bloomfield first gives an articulatory definition of the vowel,[62] then later states that it is convenient to use this and other terms in different ways and to supplement them for description of individual languages.[63] He proceeds to demonstrate convincingly the way the phonemicist can define his flexible terms to fit a particular language; his sample is English.[64]

No other phonetic dichotomy entails so many difficulties as consonant–vowel division; articulatory and acoustic criteria are there so thoroughly entwined with contextual and strictural function and problems of segmentation that only a rigid descriptive order will sep-

[62] Bloomfield, *Lang.*, 102.   [63] *Ibid.*, 102 n.   [64] *Ibid.*, 130.

arate them. Once granted this order, however, further criteria fit the pattern quite readily for the remainder of phonetic classifications; lacking it, difficulties initiating at this point carry clear through a system.[65]

Criteria for various series of sound types need no detailed discussion at this point; most of them have been given directly or by implication. Nasals as distinguished from stops and vowels have already been mentioned (with cavity function separating nasals from vowels); fricative or frictionless laterals are characterized by front contact and side opening, in contrast to the side contact and front opening of central fricative and frictionless continuants; oral fricatives are separated from vowels by an acoustic criterion; affricates and diphthongs break up phonetically into individually described segments.

One further item merits some mention. Some articulators, especially the tip of the tongue, can touch at more than one point, for example, the teeth, or the dome of the mouth. For many sounds it proves more convenient to assume a norm in which an articulator touches a certain spot (e.g. back of tongue on velum). Sweet comments that an alphabet could use separate signs for these factors,[66] although in general he does not attempt such detail; Jespersen criticizes Bell's visible speech for not doing so,[67] and then provides for them in his own analphabetic system. Choice of such representation, along with the number of points of articulation to be shown in basic symbols, seems to be a question of practical rather than theoretical limits.[68] If such a term as " labiodental " is to be used to show an articulator in relation to its point of articulation, then, obviously enough, " labiovelar " should not appear in the same series with it.

[65] Cf. Jespersen, *Articulations*, 5, for criticism of Bell's system of symbols.
[66] Sweet, 39.
[67] Jespersen, *Articulations*, 5.
[68] See Bloch and Trager, 2.

PART II

PHONETIC THEORY: A CONSTRUCTIVE SYSTEM

INTRODUCTION

IN PART I the difficulties were discussed which remain in phonetic theory because of a legacy from prephonemic days when phonetics and phonemics were one. Sounds were shown to have been chosen for description because of their use in speech rather than because of their articulatory or acoustic nature; many sounds were seen to have been ignored because they were not produced in a certain way; classifications had numerous basic assumptions behind them which were not apparent since the contrastive data were not given due attention.

In Part II of this study a phonetic classification is presented which should allow, with slight modifications or minor additional categories, for the analysis of all sounds — not just a group determined by non-articulatory means. This gives an opportunity to emphasize many factors which are important to phonetic theory and to contrast them with other items within a unified system. The defining of assumptions essential to such theory has made it possible to eliminate certain other assumptions related to phonemics that are undesirable here.

The phonetic materials which have served as a background for this study were collected by me during six years of investigation of living languages with informants in the field. During that time an endeavor was made to analyze and record the sounds of the following languages: Amuzgo, Aztec, Cakchiquel, Cherokee, Chinanteco, Delaware, Huaxteco, Lithuanian, Maya, Mazateco, Mixe, Mixteco, Navajo, Ojibwa, Otomi, San Blas, Spanish, Tamil, Tarascan, Tlapaneco, Totonaco, Trique, Tzeltal, and Zapateco; all but three of these (Lithuanian, Spanish, Tamil) are Indian languages of North America.

Chapter VI attempts to relate the production of the vast majority of vocal sounds to a simple set of mechanical processes which initiate, compress, rarefy, combine, or reinforce air streams. Both speech sounds and nonspeech sounds use these processes.

Chapter VII describes the methods by which the air streams are controlled and impeded so as to result in different kinds of sounds within any one major type of mechanism. The air streams passing through open cavities with as little obstruction as possible produce only weak sounds; when passageways are partly closed, however, strong sound vibrations may be set up. A discussion of the different moving parts which can cause such interference, the shapes they may assume in the process, the places at which the interference takes place, the manner in which these moving parts form the obstruction, and the resultant differences in types of sound, constitutes a considerable part of this chapter. The first section delineates the natural segmentation which was postulated in Chapter III and which proves to be conditioned by these obstructing movements. Later in the chapter the differences of strictural function which were noted in Chapter IV are given a working classification.

Chapter VIII, which concludes the study, has two main features: (1) A résumé is offered of sound types which do not seem to occur in speech. Although certain types of sound-producing mechanisms are apparently never used in phonemic systems, others may be. This forms the basis for a statement of a line of cleavage between non-speech sounds and speech sounds. (2) A summary is presented of certain features which may be described profitably for any sound to classify it by its productive mechanism and, roughly, by its controlling mechanisms. A symbol is provided for each of these factors, resulting in an analphabetic system of phonetic notation whose chief value lies in calling one's attention to the great number of assumptions which underlie our normal (and much more useful) phonetic symbols, the letters of the alphabet.

CHAPTER VI

PRODUCTIVE MECHANISMS

IN CHAPTER I the need was indicated for a theory that would show basic relationships between all types of sound mechanisms which involve compression and rarefaction. The present chapter is designed to meet that need by describing the air chambers and movements involved in various compression–rarefaction systems and to contrast these with other productive sound mechanisms.

Sounds are vibrations with characteristics of frequency, intensity, and duration which produce certain sensations of audibility when impinging upon the ear. Sound waves may be set up in the physical world in a variety of ways. A few of these methods concern us here: One object striking against another, as when a hammer hits an anvil, sets up vibrations. One object scraping or rubbing against a second may likewise cause sound waves, as when a pen scratches on paper. A blast of air may be set in vibration by going over a sharp ledge or through a narrow orifice, as when air escapes from an automobile tire. The air may put an object in vibration, as does the breath of a clarinet player the reed of his instrument. A body of air may vibrate, as does a resonance chamber below a tuning fork. Vibrations may travel from one medium to another; the dropping of a book in one room may be heard in another as sound waves travel through the partition and induce vibrations in the adjoining room. All these methods can be discovered in the production of vocal sound, although a large majority of the sounds utilize a moving column of air.

AIR-STREAM MECHANISMS

Within the vocal apparatus there are five *cavities* (see Fig. 1). These embrace the *oral, nasal, pharyngeal, pulmonic,* and *esophageal* (including the stomach) cavities. A back velar (or uvular) closure is considered to be within, but terminating, the oral cavity; analogously, a velic closure (" velic " used, as in Part I, to indicate the upper part of the velum facing the nasopharynx) lies within the nasal cavity;

glottal and esophageal closures are contained within the pharyngeal cavity. It does not seem expedient to attempt to work with a classification which would separate the laryngeal and pharyngeal cavities, or the esophageal and stomach cavities.

Any cavity or part of a cavity which is completely shut off by itself from others by some closure, or any group of cavities or parts of

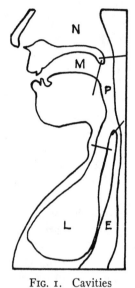

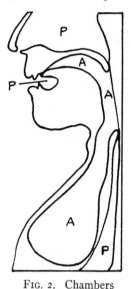

Fig. 1. Cavities

E, esophagus; L, lungs; M, mouth; N, nose; P, pharynx

Fig. 2. Chambers

A, parts of the active chamber; P, passive chambers. The sound is [t]

cavities which are united by connecting passageways of air, forms an *air chamber*. Thus, during the stop [p] there are three air chambers: the nasal, the oral-pharyngeal-pulmonic, the esophageal. With a nasalized vowel [a], only two air chambers are present: the esophageal and the oral-nasal-pharyngeal-pulmonic. With [n] there are three: esophageal, front oral, and (back) oral-nasal-pharyngeal-pulmonic.

The air chamber in specific use for a particular sound, the one which contains the air stream, is the *active* chamber (see Figs. 2–3, 9). All other chambers are *passive* (see Figs. 2–3). In the examples given in the preceding paragraph the esophageal chamber was always passive. The nasal chamber is passive for all oral sounds; the oral and nasal chambers are passive for glottal stop. During [p] the oral-pharyngeal-pulmonic chamber is active, and so on.

When one is describing sequences of segments, another term is convenient too. A passive chamber is also *semipassive* (see Fig. 7) when due to become active during the next sound. With [k] the oral cham-

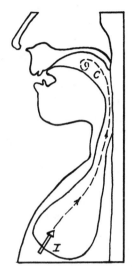

FIG. 4. Capped air stream

C, air stream; *I*, initiator. The sound is [t]

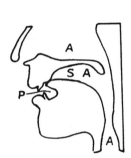

FIG. 3. Side chamber

A, active chamber; *P*, passive chamber; *S*, side chamber. The sound is [n]

ber (the part in front of the closure) is passive, but in [k] followed by [w] or [a] it is at the same time semipassive, since after the velar release air will be passing through the oral cavity and making it active.

When part of an active air chamber does not have the air stream passing directly through it, but only by it, that part becomes a *side chamber* (see Fig. 3). This is seen almost exclusively during the production of front nasals such as [m] or [n]. The air comes from the lungs out through the nose, but does not pass directly through the mouth even though the mouth has direct connection with the pulmonic, pharyngeal, and nasal cavities and affects the total resonance of the sound.

Certain parts of the walls of an air chamber may be flexible: any part is an *initiator* (see Figs. 4–10) of an air stream at the time the part is moving within the chamber, making the chamber smaller or larger. The bellows of an accordion constitute an initiator; the total air chamber is made larger and smaller by its movement, and this movement initiates the air stream which vibrates the reeds. The lungs are the most frequently used initiator in the production of vocal sound. Other initiators are the moving larynx, tongue, lips, esophagus, and so on. They will be discussed separately in a moment. (All English phonemic norms are produced while the lungs function as an initiator; various clicks, and similar sounds, of African languages entail some other initiator.)

With but few exceptions, the initiator is on the inward side of its air chamber: the lungs are inward in respect to the oral and nasal cavities; the velar closure and movement of the back of the tongue are inward in respect to the oral cavity employed in clicks; and so on. In a *reversed mechanism* the initiator is outwardly situated. An example of this is the sound caused by suction when the tip of the tongue moves upward against the lower lip (see Fig. 9).

When an initiator moves toward the center of its chamber it makes the chamber smaller (contracted) and compresses the air contained therein. If there is an opening in the chamber at the mouth or nose an air stream is forced outward. All sounds made in this manner are *egressives* (or *compressives*) (see Figs. 4, 10); [m], [l], [s] are samples. If the initiator moves away from the center of its air chamber it makes the chamber larger (expanded) and produces a partial vacuum. If an opening exists in the chamber at the mouth or nose an air stream is drawn inward. Sounds made thus are *ingressives* (or *rarefactives*) (cf. Figs. 5–8); ingressive lung-air sounds, and clicks, are produced in this way.

If no opening at the mouth or the nose is provided for compressives (e.g. stops [p], [t], [k]), an air stream is initiated which continues only until the pressure is equalized throughout the entire chamber. Pressure of the lungs in [b], for example, may force enough air into the mouth through the glottis to vibrate the vocal cords for a moment, but as soon as the pressure in the mouth equals that of the lungs, no more air will pass the vocal cords (and hence vibration will cease) unless the cheeks are expanded to provide further place for entrance of air or unless the velic or labial closure is released (which, of course,

changes the stop into a continuant). In such a situation, either before or after the equalization of pressure, the air stream is *capped*
(see Fig. 4). With rarefactive stops the situation is in reverse. The
air stream persists in the direction of the lowest pressure area until
the pressures are equalized.

An initiator with its full gamut of possible air chambers is an *air-
stream mechanism,* or, more briefly, an *air mechanism* (see Figs. 5–6).
The initiator with the adjacent part of the air chamber constitutes the
bellows, but the remainder of the air chamber provides the pipes or
keys. Just as a musical instrument does not have to employ every
key or pipe at the same time, so an air mechanism may for a single
sound use just a small part of the space of its potential air chambers.

Any air chamber, even if passive, is a *potential air-stream mechanism,* since the addition of an initiator would turn it into an active
air mechanism. The mouth cavity, for example, which is passive during the closure for [k], is a potential air mechanism since it would
produce some type of click if the tongue should move backward to
initiate an ingressive oral air stream.

Three air-stream mechanisms may be considered to be *major* types,
as contrasted with several *minor* ones, since the former can produce
many kinds of sounds and series of sounds, whereas the latter are
extremely limited in productive possibilities (although the esophageal
type is limited less than other minor mechanisms).

MAJOR AIR-STREAM MECHANISMS

Pulmonic Air-Stream Mechanism

The lungs acting as an initiator may press *lung air* outward through
the pharynx and mouth or nose (or some connected combination).
This may be done in a rapid burst, as after a cough, where the pressure
is obvious, or very slowly, as for a sustained frictionless continuant
whose pressure is slight but which may be continued for about half
a minute. During inspiration the enlarging of this chamber may likewise be rapid or sustained, the time being limited by the capacity
of the lungs to continue expansion. For a diagrammatic indication
of the movement of the initiator and the air stream in [t] see Figure 4.

More sound types can be produced with lung air than with any
other mechanism. All English phonemic norms use egressive lung

air only. Both egressive and ingressive stops, fricatives, frictionless spirants, vocoids, trills (most ingressive trills are extremely difficult to produce and differ acoustically and structurally from egressive types), laterals, and so on,[1] can be produced by this mechanism.

In order to show the interaction and interdependence of initiators, air streams, and certain typical strictures, and the simultaneous action of several mechanisms, the following symbols are presented, which apply throughout the sample diagrams here and later. The diagrams are to be read from left to right. When [h] is given, its purpose is to allow demonstration of releases and so on; the sound is assumed for convenience to be a type of voiceless vocoid which has the tongue flat in the mouth and, therefore, no vocoidal partial stricture.

l	lips	→→→→	movement (of air stream or initiator) outward
b	back part of tongue		
v	velic		
g	glottis	←←←←	movement inward
w	wall of lungs	L	lung air
———	closure	P	pharynx air
– – – –	fricative stricture	M	mouth air
, , , ,	frictionless stricture	c c c c	capped compressive air stream
. . . .	zero stricture		
⌇⌇⌇	vibration	r r r r	capped rarefactive air stream

```
        [hph]                    [u]              Ingressive [χ]
l  . . ———— . .          l  , , , ,            l  . . . .
b  . . . . . . . .        b  , , , ,            b  _ _ _ _
v  ————————               v  ————               v  ————
g  . . . . . . . .        g  ⌇⌇⌇⌇               g  . . . .
w  →→→→→→→→                w  →→→→               w  ←←←←
L  →→cccc→→                L  →→→→               L  ←←←←
```

Pharyngeal Air-Stream Mechanism

The larynx with glottis closed (but for voiced types see combinations with lung air) may be thrust upward, compressing the air beyond it. If an egress is provided through the mouth or nose *pharynx air* will rush out. When there is no egress, a pharyngeal

---

[1] In this chapter these terms will be used with their traditional meanings. In Chapter VII certain of them will be redefined in slightly different ways. A "vocoid" is an articulatory approximation of a vowel; a "contoid" is such an approximation for a consonant. For their further definition, and for a contextual redefinition of "vowel" and "consonant," see pp. 143–45.

capped air stream results; these are *glottalized stops* (the " ejectives " of British usage, or the " glottalic pressure stops " of Catford). The larynx may likewise be lowered, rarefying the air in that section of the chamber, and setting up an ingressive air stream to fill the gap. Stops of this nature are *implosives* (described by some writers as " glottalic clicks," or " glottalic suction stops "). See Figure 5 for a diagram of this mechanism.

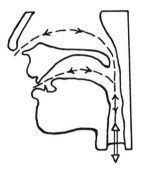 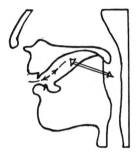

FIG. 5. Pharyngeal air mechanism FIG. 6. Oral air mechanism

The long arrows show potential initiator movement; the broken lines show potential movement of pharyngeal air streams (Fig. 5) and of oral air streams (Fig. 6)

Sounds with pharynx air include the same general types as with lung air, subject to certain changes and limitations. The comparison does not cease with stops, but includes fricatives, frictionless spirants, vocoids, and the like. Egressive pharynx-air sounds have *glottalized timbre;* ingressive, *implosive timbre.* Because of the weakness and shortness of duration of the air stream, which even with a fricative stricture can be maintained for only a few seconds, the majority of pharynx-air frictionless continuants tend to have zero audibility. The whistles, frictionless trills, and lip " voice " (see p. 126) provide occasional exceptions. The most frequent exceptions are the *percussive-transition pharynx-air vocoids* (see pp. 93–94, 104, 115), which constitute the loud " pop " due to the front oral release of nonaffricated clicks (or even weaker sounds following the release of some close fricatives). For the sounds commonly called " glottalized vowels " (not made with pharynx air) see the discussion of laryngealization on pages 127–28. All sounds with this mechanism are, in the nature of the case, completely voiceless, since voice is a function of the vocal cords during the action of the pulmonic mechanism (combinations of the two mechanisms will receive attention below, pp. 94–96). Lip " voice " (see p. 126), however, is clearly audible. Modifications such as labialization produce audible effects upon the release of stops and upon fricatives; lip rounding as a primary articulation, if it is to be audible by itself without other strictures, has to be of the fricative, or else the whistle, type. Certain whistles produced by pharynx air are readily audible, even if brief. Certain trills (e.g. alveolar) can be made with this mechanism, but others (e.g. full bilabial) are difficult since they require a heavy air stream. No sound types can be made by this mechanism alone which with pulmonic mechanism would demand any kind of complete or partial glottal stricture (e.g. glottal stop, or whisper), since the glottis is already closed as initiator and needs strictures of other functions beyond it for sound production; the vibrating glottis in voiced types is not a function of this mechanism.

Velar glottalized stop, plus [h]	*Bilabial implosive fricative*	*Velic glottalized fricative*
l	l _ _ _ _	l _____
b _____. . . .	b	b . . . .
v _____	v _____	v _ _ _ _
g →→→→→→. .	g ←←←←	g →→→→
w →→	P ←←←←	P →→→→
L →→		
P c c c c →→		

Three further diagrams are given to illustrate types of release of a velar glottalized stop: (1) affricated, and with quick glottal release, (2) affricated, but with slow glottal release, (3) nonaffricated, but followed by a percussive-transition glottalized vocoid and then delayed glottal release. Already illustrated above is the type which is nonaffricated and followed by a percussive-transition glottalized vocoid and then quick glottal release.

k' x' A	k' x' ʔ A	k' A' ʔ A
l	l	l . . . .
b _____ _ _	b _____ _ _.	b _____. . . . .
v _____	v _____	v _____
g →→→→→→. . . .	g →→→→→→———. . . .	g →→→→→→———. . . .
w (→→→→) →→→→	w (→→→→) →→→→→→	w (→→→→) →→→→→→
L (c c c c) →→→→	L (c c c c) c c→→→→	L (c c c c) c c→→→→
P c c c c →→	P c c c c→→	P c c c c→→

Oral Air-Stream Mechanism

The back part of the tongue while touching the velum may be thrust forward, compressing any *mouth air* caught between it and some stricture farther forward, at the tongue tip or lips or the like; if a place of escape is provided, an egressive air stream is produced. The back part of the tongue may be moved farther back in the mouth while maintaining its velar closure and in this manner rarefy the air in the chamber and initiate an ingressive stream to the mouth; the sounds of kissing, or of clucking to horses, are produced in this way.

This mechanism (see Fig. 6) is used for sucking water up into a straw; the rarefaction of the oral cavity allows air pressure to push the cheeks in simultaneously. If one has his mouth full of water and ejects the liquid forcibly a distance of a few feet, a modified form of the egressive oral mechanism is being used. That neither the suction nor the pressure is derived from the lungs in these experiments can be demonstrated by breathing out from or into the lungs by the nose at the same time; the oral cavity is a separate unit. A nursing baby uses a type of ingressive oral mechanism, but with certain peristaltic modifications in tongue movement which are not pertinent to sound production.

Like the pharyngeal air mechanism, the oral one has small expansion–contraction powers. Sounds produced by it rarely last more than a fraction of a second, though their spirants can be continued weakly for a second or two.

Subject to the following limitations, sounds of the oral air mechanism comprise the same stop, fricative, frictionless spirant, and vocoid types as those produced by lung air: sounds with ingressive mouth air have *click timbre;* with egressive air, *egressive-click timbre* (but in contrast to lung-air and pharynx-air sounds, the ingressives are the more common in speech). Only sounds produced by oral strictures may occur with this mechanism, since the pharyngeal and nasal cavities are completely outside it (except following velar release); nasalized or voiced types are achieved only in combination with the pulmonic mechanism. Mouth-air frictionless continuants tend to have zero audibility except for whistles, frictionless trills, lip " voice " (see p. 126), and percussive-transition click vocoids (see pp. 91, 104–5, 115), which usually (that is, except for affricated clicks) constitute the loud " pop " in the instant following the front oral release of a click stop. When the velar closure releases first, at the end of a click stop, or forms a fricative partial stricture at the same time that it is moving as an initiator, egress or ingress of the air stream is by way of the pharynx or nose.

A kiss	Bilabial click fricative	Bilabial egressive-click stop, plus [h]
1 _____ . .	1 _ _ _ _	1 _____ . . . .
b ←←←←←←	b ←←←←	b →→→→→→ . .
M r r r r ←←	M ←←←←	v —
		g . .
		w →→
		L →→
		M c c c c →→

For types of vocoidal or affricated releases one may draw analogies from pharynx-air diagrams (see p. 92).

Certain differences of tongue position may modify the character of the oral air mechanism. Although the air chambers may be quite similar, the initiator may at various times comprise larger or smaller sections of the wall of the chamber. Parts of the tongue other than the back portion may make the closing contact, be raised and fronted, backed and lowered, in conjunction with it; the mid section may be lowered while the back part is relatively stationary and still produce effects similar to the type in which the back part of the tongue is moving.

In fact, a number of very loud and sharp click stops come from a type of oral mechanism whose air chamber is zero, since the whole surface of the tongue is in close contact with the roof of the mouth. The initiator is the lowering, backing, and contracting tongue in its entirety (if we ignore the root of the tongue outside the oral cavity), except that a back point retains contact on the velum. From this type of mechanism no egressive sounds can emerge since within the zero air chamber there lies no air to be compressed.

COMBINATIONS OF MAJOR AIR-STREAM MECHANISMS

Three major mechanisms have been listed: pulmonic, pharyngeal, oral. Since their productive initiators are separately placed, with relatively independent muscle systems, they can function simultaneously if the air chambers needed by each can either be kept separate or serve in two functions at the same time. The pulmonic mechanism, for example, usually includes the oral cavity within its active air chambers; for the oral cavity to become an oral mechanism at the same time, therefore, the pulmonic mechanism must either confine itself to air chambers which do not include that cavity or else manage to use it concomitantly. A statement of possible combinatory types follows.

Pharyngeal Mechanism plus Pulmonic Mechanism

The pharyngeal mechanism in its normal function requires a closed glottis, so that when the larynx is raised or lowered compression or rarefaction may follow. If the glottis were wide open no pharyngeal compression or rarefaction would take place, and the only modification of the pulmonic sound would be caused by the expansion or contraction of the pharyngeal cavity as part of its air chamber; no air stream would be initiated in the pharynx.

On the other hand, the only pulmonic sound which can be made with glottal closure is the glottal stop. This might appear to prohibit entirely any combination of the two mechanisms.

The rarefaction developed by the laryngeal movement, however, is slightly more than is needed for the sounds of the pharyngeal mechanism. A slight leakage of air from the lungs through the glottis may be sufficient to vibrate the vocal cords, while not destroying the partial vacuum produced by the lowering larynx which sucks air into the mouth and pharynx. This produces the sounds [ɓ], [ɗ], and the like (see Fig. 8), often known as " implosives." For a mechanical illustration by stream cylinders see Catford in *Le Maître Phonétique*, 3d Series, 65 (1939), 4.

Since under these conditions the pharyngeal and oral cavities constitute the air chamber for the pharyngeal mechanism and at the same time constitute the outer part of the air chamber for the pulmonic mechanism, two descriptions would at first seem to be possible: ingressive pharynx-air stops or fricatives could be said to be accompanied by voice or else voiced lung-air stops and fricatives might be said to be modified by an ingressive air stream to the pharynx. The choice of the first description is made because the glottis functioning as vibrator is given a lower place in the descriptive rank of structural function (see pp. 130–31, 133) than are the oral strictures prominent to the implosion.

Three other types of combination are much more difficult to produce, and sometimes the results are of doubtful validity. Voicing by egressive pulmonic air can be added to egressive (instead of ingressive) pharynx air. This produces voiced glottalized stops and fricatives. Here again the use of " glottalized " timbre to designate egressive pharynx air is different from the general practice; certain sequences of (apparently fortis) glottal stop followed by voiced spirants at times combine to constitute single phonemes and are called " glottalized voiced spirants " by a number of writers.[2] The combination into single phonemes of a glottal stop with other sounds in sequence might by the phonemicist be conveniently termed " sequential glottalization," in contradistinction to the pharynx-air type.

An ingressive voiced stop is difficult to produce with lung air. This difficulty is amplified when one tries to combine voicing from ingressive lung air with either egressive or ingressive pharynx-air stops. With the fricatives the difficulty is slightly less, but sufficiently formidable, so that I have thus far failed to produce many of the types postulated by these analogies.

The mechanisms can be combined a bit more readily at times if, instead of voice, a glottal trill is substituted in each case, whether with ingressive or egressive lung air. The reason for this appears to be that a glottal trill uses a much smaller air stream than does voice and hence does not so quickly destroy the pharyngeal vacuum for ingressive pharynx-air types or add excessive pressure for egressive ones; correlated with this is the fact that the glottal formation seems to approach nearer to a position of closure than for voice (and for the same reason decreases the size of the air stream). The relation of glottal trill to voice will be discussed briefly in the next chapter (pp. 126–28).

[6h]	Implosive [ß]	Sequential glottalization of [ß] (i.e. [ʔß])
l ———	l _ _ _ _	l _ _ _ _ _ _
b	b	b . . . . . .
v ———————	v ———	v ———
g ⋘⋘⋘ · ·	g ⋘⋘	g ～～～
w ⇢⇢⇢⇢⇢⇢⇢	w ⇢⇢⇢⇢	w ⇢⇢⇢⇢⇢⇢
L c c c c⇢⇢⇢	L ⇢⇢⇢⇢	L c c⇢⇢⇢⇢
P r r r r⇇	P ⇇⇇⇇	

[2] Cf. Sapir, " Glottalized Continuants in Navaho, Nootka, and Kwakiutl (with a Note on Indo-European)," *Lang.*, 14 (1938), 248–74.

Oral Mechanism plus Pulmonic Mechanism

During the production of any mouth-air sound lung air of either ingressive or egressive type may cause simultaneous phenomena. The entire range of ingressive or egressive clicks can be produced under these conditions, but the lung-air sounds are limited to types which can be completely executed behind a velar closure, using pulmonic,

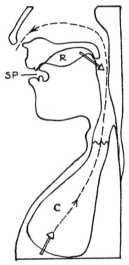 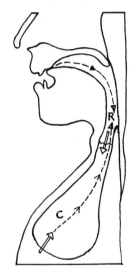

FIG. 7. Alveolar click stop with   FIG. 8.   Voiced alveolar implo-
    voiced nasalization   sive stop

C, compression; R, rarefaction; SP, semipassive chamber; ~ vibrating
    vocal cords; arrows and dotted lines show the direction of movement
    of initiators and air streams
The sound represented in Figure 7 precedes an oral release

pharyngeal, and nasal cavities; the velar closure may do double duty — as initiator for the clicks, but as oral closure for the lung-air sounds.

Sounds known as nasalized clicks (see Fig. 7) have simultaneous [ŋ]; voiced clicks have simultaneous [g]; the air stream in this second type is capped at one exit by the velic closure and at the other by the whole oral click mechanism, but specifically by its velar closure-initiator. Various types of releases can be given; if the click releases first, then the velar closure can release as for a normal [g], and so on.

The vocal cords do not, of course, need to be vibrating for these combinations, so that the pulmonic contribution could be voiceless. Since the oral and pulmonic mechanisms have separate initiators and may use separate air chambers, their air streams do not have to be both egressive or both ingressive at the same time. All four possible combinations can readily be given: ingressive lung air plus ingressive mouth air; egressive lung air plus egressive mouth air; ingressive lung air plus egressive mouth air; egressive lung air plus ingressive mouth air.

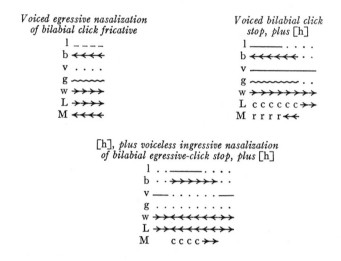

Oral Mechanism plus Pharyngeal Mechanism

To any egressive click may be added a velic glottalized fricative or a velic-released velar glottalized stop; to any (ingressive) click may be added a velic implosive fricative or a velic-released velar implosive stop. Apparently the direction of the air streams must be the same, either both egressive or both ingressive; this has nothing to do with the theoretical possibility of ingressive pharynx air plus egressive mouth air, and vice versa, as far as the air chambers are concerned; it appears to be simply a limitation of muscular arrangements such that it is physiologically difficult to be lowering the larynx while fronting the tongue. Perhaps the mechanical difficulty can be overcome; if so, the velic glottalized fricative can be made to accompany an ingressive click, and so on. All these sounds are in the nature of the case voiceless, since voicing implies pulmonic mechanism for vocal-cord vibration.

Velic-released velar glottalized stop with simultaneous bilabial egressive-click fricative, plus [h]

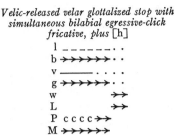

Oral Mechanism plus Pharyngeal Mechanism plus Pulmonic Mechanism

The sounds described in the preceding paragraph can be voiced by having a leakage of lung air vibrate the cords during the movement of the pharyngeal initiator. The difficulties of voicing during ingressive lung air are here accentuated to such an extent by the extra mechanisms that of eight possible ingressive–egressive combination types I have succeeded in making sounds of one or two only.

Voiced velic-released velar implosive stop with simultaneous bilabial click stop, plus [h]

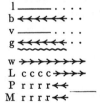

MINOR AIR-STREAM MECHANISMS

The esophagus can be expanded or contracted as an initiator of *esophagus air,* with sounds both ingressive and egressive. The remnant of the air chamber is the same as for lung-air sounds except that the pulmonic cavity is not included. A modification of this type entails use of the stomach, also, as initiator and part of the air chamber; compressive types may be made by gas. The esophageal mechanism is employed principally for making belches.

The esophageal mechanism can be used to produce a large percentage of the sound types that are seen in the pulmonic mechanism. Each of the sounds is modified by *belch timbre*. Many of the sound types, however, cannot be distinguished from one another acoustically since the belch timbre itself masks out numerous distinctive features which could otherwise be observed. The opening into the esophagus serves as a vibrator analogous to the vocal cords; it is difficult if not impossible to eliminate its vibration entirely in order to obtain sounds perfectly analogous to pulmonic voiceless types.

Combinations can be made between the esophageal mechanism and the oral or pharyngeal one. To obtain descriptions of them one can use previous descriptions of combinations of the pulmonic type with oral and pharyngeal mechanisms, substituting esophageal mechanism and vibration for the pulmonic type with voice. One added combination must be mentioned: during the belches air may be escaping from the lungs to vibrate the vocal cords and add true voicing to the belched stops, fricatives, or vocoids.

Laryngectomized patients are sometimes taught to use esophagus air as a substitute for the lung air which no longer passes through the supraglottal cavities. There is some question about the vibrator as the voicing substitute in this instance; the claim that the epiglottis serves for this is open to question.[3] I have had no opportunity to study the voices of such persons directly, but from a sound film [4] it appears that any one " breath group " is limited to perhaps ten syllables in the most expert speakers, who use esophagus air perhaps exclusively. Less expert speakers use fewer syllables and supplement esophagus air with pharynx air for making many voiceless sounds, especially stops.

There is a large group of other minor mechanisms, but none of them can produce a great variety of sounds; they are limited to a very few stops and fricatives each, with or without lip rounding and with other minute modifications.

[3] Cf. Morrison and Fineman ("Production of Pseudo-voice after Total Laryngectomy," *Trans. Am. Acad. Ophthalmol. and Otolaryngol.*, 41 [1936], 631) for a statement of various types of vibrators used by these laryngectomized patients. Jackson ("The Voice after Direct Laryngoscopic Operations, Laryngofissure and Laryngectomy," *Arch. of Otolaryngol.*, 31 [1940], 35) doubts the value of the epiglottis as a vibrator.

[4] See p. 25, n. 97.

If the tongue tip is turned down under the tongue in such a way that the blade of the tongue touches the lower lip, the separation of the tongue (by moving the blade farther back into the mouth) from the lip produces a suction sound, an ingressive stop.

If the lower lip is pulled somewhat into the mouth up over the lower teeth and the tip of the tongue is then placed against the lower

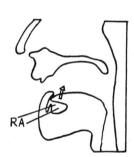

FIG. 9.   Minor reversed air mechanism

A, active air chamber; *R*, rarefaction. The arrow shows the direction of movement of the initiator

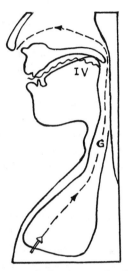

FIG. 10.   Induction mechanism

G, vibrating vocal cords; *IV*, induced vibrator; ∿ induced train of sound waves

teeth and gradually slid up across and off from the lower lip, a different type of suction sound may be noted (see Fig. 9) ; the mechanism is of the reversed type.

Several varieties of minor mechanisms may be discovered by manipulating the tongue in various ways in the bottom of the mouth.

These minor mechanisms can be combined with a large number of lung-air sounds and a few pharynx-air and mouth-air sounds; the sounds of the major mechanisms which may combine with these mechanisms are in general those which do not need the front part of the tongue in their articulation.

The tongue tip may be used in several other ways, in the upper part of the mouth rather than the lower. It may, for example, be placed outside but against the upper teeth, while touching the upper lip. If the tongue tip and lip are then opened outward, while the blade is moved inward, the blade serves as an initiator for ingressive sounds. This mechanism is used frequently to suck the teeth to remove food particles and the like; in this capacity it is also to be observed in a modification which places the tongue tip up between the teeth and the cheek at the side of the mouth.

If two closures are made by the tongue, one at the velum and the other at the alveolar arch, the movement backward of the back part of the tongue causes rarefaction of the air between the two closures. But if the tip of the tongue is moved backward it compresses the air in that chamber; a release of the tip then allows egressive escape of compressed air. Since the initiator is at the front of the chamber, the mechanism is of the reversed type.

When the mouth cavity is almost completely closed by the tongue (approximately in position for [t]), a zero cavity with small boundaries is left between the teeth and cheeks. If the cheeks are drawn outward by the fingers they may serve as initiators for rarefactive sounds. If the cheeks are first puffed out (with pharynx air or mouth air), so that the cavity between the teeth and cheeks is filled with air, the cheeks may then by their own power serve as initiators of compressive sounds by forcing themselves toward the teeth to drive out the air from the cavity.

Similar sounds can be made by the lips. The oral cavity may be closed with the tongue, while the space between the lips and teeth is puffed full of air, after which the lips as initiator can be forced in toward the teeth to make compressive sounds. Since the initiator here is on the outward edge of the air chamber, the mechanism is another reversed one. A modification of this mechanism can produce a rarefactive sound or two. With the oral cavity closed by the tongue, the closed lips are thrust sharply outward and then opened; a slight rarefactive sound is heard. The reverse of this may produce a slight compressive sound.

Like other mechanisms, these can enter into various combinations. Their sounds can be produced simultaneously with those of pulmonic, oral, and pharyngeal major mechanisms, or even with other minor mechanisms, provided the various initiators, air chambers, points of articulation, and articulators do not overlap in such a way as to prevent for mechanical reasons the combination of types already illustrated.

PERCUSSION MECHANISMS

Just at the time some part of the wall of an air chamber is making or breaking a closure it becomes a *percussor,* if there is no centering or outward movement in respect to the chamber during the actual contact time. Percussors differ from initiators in several ways: in opening and closing they move perpendicularly to the entrance of the air chamber, instead of having a section of the wall of an air chamber move for some time toward or away from the center of the chamber; they produce no directional air current, but merely a disturbance that starts sound waves which are modified by certain cavity resonators; they manifest their releasing or approaching *percussive timbre* only at the moments of the opening and closing of some passage, with no possibility of producing protracted compression or rarefaction of air and no possibility of continuous sound production.

When the lips open or close, they are percussors. The tip of the tongue making closure on the alveolar arch is one likewise. The velic closing the nasal passage, the tongue closing the oral cavity at the velum, the vocal cords snapping together for a glottal stop are all illustrations of percussive action. Children frequently make a lingual percussive by slapping the tongue sharply against the floor of the mouth; this is usually done as part of the release movement of a lingual click.[5]

Certain percussives tend to be below the threshold of audibility unless two conditions are present: (1) the movement must usually be rather sharp, forceful, and rapid; (2) the chamber of which they are a part must be a completely enclosed body of air, as for a stop.

The majority of relatively loud types are made by front oral percussors when there is a velar closure or when there is both glottal and velic closure. This can be seen by making the lips open and close in rapid forceful sequence under the following varied conditions: first with the glottal and nasal passages open as for a nasalized vowel

---

[5] Doke ("An outline of the Phonetics of the Language of the Čhũ: Bushmen of North-West Kalahari," *Bantu Studies,* 2, No. 3 [1925], 163) reports such a click as an abnormality of one speaker.

(this usually gives but very slight noise, or no audible noise); then with velic closure (still almost inaudible, probably entirely so for the releasing percussive); next with glottal and velic closures (immediately audible, for both releasing and approaching percussor); finally, with oral closures at the velum or farther front (still definitely audible). An interesting experiment substantiates the validity of this series. Form the same cavities, with the same series of closures; instead of closing the lips, snap the cheek sharply with the finger. For the type with glottal closure one may obtain similar results by snapping the throat instead of the cheek. When the lips are open during this snapping the result is similar to the sound of releasing percussives; the latter tend to sound briefly vocoidal. If the lips are closed the results are more like the closing percussives or like the action of a drum when beaten.

Air chambers which have percussors but no initiators are *percussion mechanisms* and have *static air* rather than an air stream. Any passive chamber is a potential percussion mechanism, since it becomes an active one if a percussor is added.

Certain of the percussion mechanisms can enter into combination with each other, just as can the air mechanisms. In such groupings, however, the oral percussors are usually the only ones audible. If, for example, the glottis, velum, velic, and lips are closed, the release of the latter two simultaneously usually leaves only the labial one audible.

Percussors and their sounds may be added to all air streams, however. The closures and releases of all stops are caused by the addition of percussors to air streams. The closures at the start of [p], [t], and [k] may be distinctly audible if made sharply enough. On the release it is impossible at times to separate the sound of the percussor from that of the releasing compressed air. In lung-air sounds the releasing percussive is usually inaudible, as we have already stated, so one would hardly expect to hear it when the sound of the releasing air is produced at the same time. In pharynx-air and mouth-air sounds this difficulty is nonexistent, but a new one is added: the release of the capped air stream often seems to exaggerate the sound of the releasing percussive rather than to make a new sound of its own. The release of certain very loud sharp-cut glottalized stops gives the acoustic impression of releasing percussives only, except for being louder. (Some percussive-transition vocoids have already been discussed; see pp. 91, 93.)

Percussion mechanisms as a whole can enter into combination with air mechanisms. One example of this is seen when velar closure and bilabial percussive form an oral percussion mechanism with static air, while the lungs, as initiator for a pulmonic air mechanism, thrust air out through the nose and vibrating glottis; the opening and closing of the lips are clearly audible above the sound of the voiced nasal (but compare the induction mechanisms, p. 106). Double stops are sometimes built up in a way similar to this. The pulmonic mechanism gives a pulmonic air stream which vibrates the vocal cords and is capped by velic and velar closures; the oral cavity has no air stream since the back part of the tongue is stationary, but the cavity is turned into a percussion mechanism by the release of the lips. This bilabial percussive is added to the sound of the voiced [g]. After the labial release the velar closure may release also in the normal manner of a releasing voiced velar stop. The grouping of such items into single phonemes is a linguistic feature beyond the scope of this discussion.

Bilabial releasing concussion   *Double stop* [bg],
of pharyngeal static air   *plus* [h]

    l _____ . .   l _____ . . . . . .
    b . . . . . .   b _____ . .
    v _____   v _____
    g _____   g ∿∿∿∿∿∿∿ . .
                                               w →→→→→→→→→→→
                                               L c c c c c c c c c →→

SCRAPING MECHANISMS

Sounds caused by the rubbing of one object against another are very rare in vocal types. A few *scrapives* may be found, however, which are produced in this way. The lower teeth being rubbed back and forth against the upper ones may produce one such sound. Another can be made by scraping the lower teeth up and down against the inside of the lower lip. All such sounds are distinct from *fricatives* (see p. 141), which are caused by friction of air streams.

INDUCTION MECHANISMS

If sound vibrations (from voicing, primarily) are transmitted across some closure or wall of a chamber, that section becomes an *induced vibrator* for sounds of static air in an *induction mechanism* (see Fig. 10). Such sounds are initiated in an active chamber but have their vibrations carried across the chamber wall into a passive one. If during the continuous pronunciation of a voiced velar nasal the lips are repeatedly opened and partly closed (but not completely closed, or percussives will result also; see p. 103), changing induced resonances may be detected. If the velic is perfectly closed for the production of oral sounds, any vibrations which may be present in the nasal cavity are likewise due to an induction mechanism.

This chapter has shown that most sounds entail the use of some type of air stream. Air streams may be either egressive or ingressive. Exactly halfway between egressive or ingressive types lie the percussion mechanisms; if some part of the chamber wall of a percussion mechanism begins to move inward or outward, especially the lungs, glottal closure, or velar closure, the mechanism immediately becomes an active air type. The following chapter will show how the air streams initiated in air-stream mechanisms are controlled and modified.

CHAPTER VII

CONTROLLING MECHANISMS

SEGMENTATION

IN CHAPTER III (pp: 42–55) there was discussed the possibility of cutting a continuum into phonetic segments which would not be phonemes but would reflect a natural segmentation of vocal sound production. At this point a statement will be presented delimiting such segments, after which the various factors involved will be considered separately.

Statement: A *segment* is a sound (or lack of sound) having indefinite borders but with a center that is produced by a crest or trough of stricture during the even motion or pressure of an initiator; in static mechanisms percussives are segmental centers.

If one says [aiaiaiaia] five troughs and four crests of stricture may be observed. A *crest* of stricture is a point in a continuum where the strictures approach more nearly a state of closure than do the strictures immediately preceding them in the sequence. The central sounds in the following groups of three have crests of stricture: [hph], [sth], [aia]. A *trough* of stricture is a point in a sequence where the strictures approach more nearly a state of openness than do the strictures immediately preceding that point. Examples are the central sounds of [php], [eai], [fhs].

The addition of any stricture adds a crest segment; illustrations: the second sounds in [hp], [nd], [ha]. The subtraction of any stricture adds a trough segment, as in [bm], [ea], [th]. The substitution of one stricture for another adds a segment, regardless of whether or not the second stricture has a greater degree of closure than the first or a different function (so long as the same air mechanism is used for each); compare [fs], [pa], [mp]. In a substitution, when one stricture is released and another added, the articulator which has the higher rank determines whether the segment is a crest or a trough. Rank of articulators constitutes a descending series: oral closure, oral fricative stricture, oral frictionless stricture, nasal stricture, pharyngeal (or glottal) stricture. Crest segments: the second sounds in [am], [os], [ap], [mp]; trough segments: the second sounds in [ma], [so], [pa], [pm]. Two strictures approaching simultaneously or two releasing simultaneously are *double* approaches and releases, but for segment production they act like single approaches and releases. Even though the two strictures of a double approach may have different structural function, the analysis remains unchanged. Double releases may be seen in [bM], [eA].[1]

The function of an initiator is such that its steady movement or pressure does not constitute a trough and crest of stricture. In a bilabial voiceless click (a kiss), for example, two units may be observed: the first unit occurs during the labial closure and the second immediately after the oral release; one does not have to add two more, one for the point at which the initiator starts moving, and another when it ceases. Nevertheless, from the articulatory point of view, the movement (or pressure after the capped air stream has equalized air pressures) of the initiator allows the voiceless stops to be classed as phonetic entities since they include the action of a phonetic mechanism.

If, however, the initiator does not move steadily, but slows down and then speeds up its movement, or decreases and then increases pressure, two unit crests will be detected. Thus if one pronounces a long continued [a], only one unit is present, but if during that sound the lungs give jerky, unsteady pressure (several chest pulses within the single qualitative sound), numerous crests of sound will constitute segment centers.

In the application of this segmentation procedure a phonetician immediately faces a complicating factor. Within the identical sequences of sound waves from a single group of articulatory movements one observer may hear a crest or trough that another investigator does not notice. Persons do not hear the same items even though listening to the same data. Certain factors contributing to this difference can be demonstrated. The longer a crest is maintained, the more readily one hears it; the louder the segment, the more likely it is to be observed. The duration and intensity of sounds influence their perceptibility. A person tends to hear things which are significant to his own

---

[1] The capital letters represent voiceless sounds.

sound system, whereas he may not notice things which are extraneous to that system: phonemic background affects one's perception of sound (e.g. a person may fail to note the presence of a glottal stop if it is not phonemic in his language). He can also hear items more readily if his attention is directed specifically toward them. Phonetic training increases the number of sounds which a person tends to notice. It does so by a contrastive procedure similar to that of phonemics in language. The instructor's ear and his marking of papers substitute for social judgment and reaction. The quality of sounds affects their perceptibility; the more two sounds resemble one another and the closer their points of articulation and types of productive mechanism, the more difficult they are to tell apart (e.g. two types of [t] which differ in production only in that one is alveolar and the other dental might be distinguished by the first of two observers but not by the second, since the sounds are acoustically very similar). The sensitivity of the mechanism recording the sounds or measuring the movements will affect the number of segments analyzed in an utterance. A deaf person will hear fewer changes in sound and stricture than will a person of normal hearing; a normal person can hear fewer sounds than can a person with exceptionally keen physiological equipment.

An *instrumental segment* is one which would be detected were instruments applied to the segmental analysis of a continuum. In this respect instruments act like ears of greater or less sensitivity; instruments of different degrees of sensitivity give different results. Every minute change of the crest or trough of stricture, resulting from the addition or subtraction of a stricture, and the like, produces a new instrumental segment even if it is below the threshold of perception, as frequently happens because of the lack of sensitivity of the ear.

When the instrumentalist has by various experiments measured the threshold of perception for strictural changes and established norms for the average ear, then *real* (or *audible*) *segments* can be delimited. A real segment is one which the average ear is physiologically capable of perceiving (i.e. after phonetic training, when its attention is directed to the segment, and when no phonemic factors interfere).

Even if the real segments in an utterance could be determined by controlled experimental conditions, phoneticians would not hear the same number of real segments under normal conditions of transcription. Differences in attention given to particular parts of a sequence, phonetic training, and phonemic background (especially the influence of one's native language) would affect the transcription. The actual outcome, therefore, is the marking off of *perceptual segments*. These are the results obtained by a phonetician who applies under normal field conditions the methodological statement already given. Just how near perceptual segments approach real segments must await an instrumental study, but the correlation apparently is quite close for trained phoneticians — close enough for perceptual segmentation to become an adequate working basis for the average situation in which phonetics is utilized. On the other hand, instrumental segmentation is frequently below the threshold for real segments; it can hinder the discovery of phonemic patterns if applied directly to the search for the phonemes themselves rather than to a description of the acoustic basis of perceptual segments and phonemes independently ascertained by linguistic technics.

Glides present a related problem. An isolated sound may have no glide at all and still be a *level segment* if there is no movement whatever of the vocal apparatus apart from that of some initiator; [s] and [f] might at times be level units. Glides must be present between segments since any approach or release involves one. The audibility of these glides varies greatly and is dependent upon much the same factors as those which influence the perceptibility of segments. The longer the duration of a glide, the slower its rate of movement, the greater the qualitative change, the greater the sensitivity of the ear, and the more a glide resembles some phonemic feature of the observer's language or some item included in his phonetic training, the greater become the possibility and probability of his hearing it. In [ia], for example, the crest and trough of stricture (the [i] and [a] respectively) may be made very long in contrast to the glide between them; in that case the glide will be practically or completely inaudible. If, however, the initial crest is of very brief duration, whereas the glide following it is relatively long, the glide will be heard by speakers of English both because of its duration and because of its significance to the consonantal phonemic pattern of English (producing [ya]).

A single-direction glide which starts at a certain position and approaches to reach a crest, or releases to reach a trough, has two segments; whether these two segmental centers are perceptual or real or instrumental will depend upon factors already discussed. A two-direction glide has at least three segments: if the stricture first moves closer and then opens, two troughs are present with one crest of stricture between them, but if the stricture first opens and then closes, a crest occurs between two troughs. Single-direction glides include [ai], [ia], [hp], [ph], [st], and the like; two-direction glides include [yae], [aia], [iai], and so on.

When the releasing (single-direction) glide of one stricture is simultaneous with the approaching glide of another, a *crossing glide* (see p. 114) is developed. If the approach be diagrammed by $/$ and the release by $\diagdown$, then the crossing glide may be diagrammed as $\times$; the central point represents a trough segment which will be perceptible in proportion to the status of the variables already mentioned for glides and perceptual segments. One such audible crossing glide is the sound of open transition between two voiceless or voiced stops; in [apta] a type of crossing-glide aspiration may be heard if the lips begin to open while the tongue is moving toward the alveolar arch (but if the first glide is completed before the second is begun, a different type of aspiration follows, a simple [h] — a trough segment, but not a crossing glide). Voiced open transition between [b] and [d] may give similar results. The crossing glide between [m] and [p] is not audible; the stopping of vocal-cord vibration and the approach for the velic closure seem to be too abrupt to allow for perceptibility of the glide. Presumably differences in structural function will at times affect the perceptibility of one or the other of the two elements in crossing glides, and will affect the perceptual segmental interpretation accordingly.

In the same way that an initiator must have steady movement (see p. 108) or else cause extra segments, so also must other strictures with different functions. If during any single-direction glide the articulator goes out of a relatively direct line to its goal, the point of greatest divergence from a direct norm constitutes a *bulge of stricture* which causes a segmental crest; see Figure 11. Thus, if during a glide from [i] to [a] the tongue sweeps backward to a mid-back position, a crest is formed between the trough for [a] and the crest for [i] which is qualitatively an unrounded back vocoid.

A *time bulge* is formed when during a glide the speed of movement is suddenly reduced (and often, but not necessarily, restored after a short interval); see Figure 12. For example, if in gliding from [a] to [i] the speed of opening is reduced as the tongue ap-

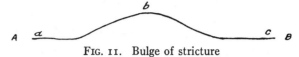

FIG. 11. Bulge of stricture

A–B, directional movement of approaching articulator; *A,*
    initial position; *B,* final position; *a,* trough; *b,* bulge;
    c, crest

proaches a mid position, a mid-front vocoid crest results. A similar time bulge may be seen in the pitch of a single vocoid. If the vocoid is begun at ' do ' and the pitch steadily (rapidly or slowly) rises toward ' sol,' two segments would be observed, first a trough (at the

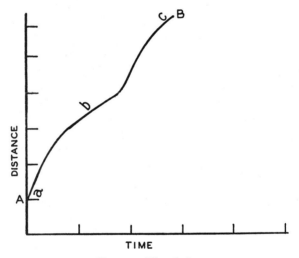

FIG. 12. Time bulge

A–B, movement of an approaching articulator; *A,* initial
    position; *B,* final position; *a,* trough; *b,* time bulge;
    c, crest

beginning) and then a crest (at the end); if during the rising glide the speed of the change of pitch should be reduced at a median point, a crest might be observed approximately at ' mi.'

When one hears a crest of sound during a release, it is sometimes difficult to determine whether the bulge is caused by change of speed or by change of the direction of movement. In a shift from [p] to [h] a quick release allows no perceptible sound between. A very slow steady release makes possible the perception of a gradual change of types of bilabial spirant, but no bulge crest. If the speed is slowed down, so that there seems to be a slight pause or hesitation of movement during this release, then one hears a crest which is some type of bilabial voiceless fricative [ø]. The process of release of the lips first and then, later, the lowering of the jaw, also adds a segment between [p] and [h], because each of the two releasing movements produces a segment.

The change from [t] to [h] presents a complication. Similar transition sounds may be observed in [th] as in [ph] (no intermediate sound audible, or steady nonsegmental audible glide, or glide crest if movement is slowed down to allow an alveolar fricative of some sort). None of these are [tsh]. If [ts] starts from identically the same position as does [t] without the sibilant, then the [s] might be considered to be formed by a bulge crest of the type which has nondirect glide (since the direct glide does not produce [s] even when slow); but it seems preferable to consider [s] a crest formed by a substituted stricture, since the section of the tongue back of the tip has to rise slightly to take its sibilant position while the tongue tip drops. If, on the other hand, the [t] starts with the blade in the exact position to anticipate the position for the [s], there will be no rise of the blade to constitute a crest. In this case one can state that the tip and blade strictures form the crest for the first segment; the tip releases to leave only the blade stricture for the second crest, and then the blade in turn releases to the trough segment [h]. This appears preferable to describing the movement as the release of the tip by an indirect route which gives a bulge heard as [s]. When one starts from a [t] which anticipates the blade position for [s] but releases both blade and tip as a whole, a fricative different in quality from any so far mentioned can be heard as a time bulge if the speed is slowed down; this fricative is quite unlike the sibilant [s] after [t]. If this whole blade section and tip are swept backward into the mouth as they descend gradually, an entirely different medial fricative crest is obtained by the nondirect movement.

It proves convenient in analyzing a sequence of segments to have names for certain types of groups. A *presequential* is composed of two segments, the second of which is, in articulatory positions, identical with the first except for one added stricture (e.g. [hp], [ai]). A *postsequential* is the reverse: a release of one stricture of the first segment produces the second (e.g. [ts], [bp], [dn]). In a *prepostsequential* the second segment is formed by an approaching stricture and the third by the release of a stricture (e.g. [aie], [sth], [abm]); a *postpresequential* is the reverse of this type. If simultaneous double releases (or approaches) are used the same terms may be applied, since in segmental delineation one is interested in locating crests and troughs of stricture, not in describing the nature of the segments. An illustration of a presequential using a double approach would be [hb], in which vocal cords and lips cause strictures at the same time. In a *prepresequential* two consecutive (not simultaneous) approaches form the second and third segments (as in [hpb]); a *postpostsequential* entails three segments with two consecutive releases producing the second and third segments (e.g. [eah]). A *substitution sequence* is composed of two crests with a crossing glide between (e.g. [pt] with rapid, but open, transition; cf., also, [eu]).

When, in a particular language, two segments combine into a single phoneme, the two segments chosen, if consonantal, are almost always in postsequential sequence; the most prominent exceptions are presequential sequences of nasal plus stop, like [nd]. Vocoid types may have diphthongs, like [ai], which are presequentials. Occasionally that which is perceptually a single segment may be two phonemes; this is frequently true of long contoids or vocoids. If voiceless stops with close transition have nothing audible during the closure, they also may be single perceptual segments working as two phonemes. Often, however, close transition of [pt] is not a single real segment, since the release of the lips gives a tiny audible percussive sound whose resonance chamber is the small static one in front of the lingual closure. In any case, this release of a stricture and the previous closure of the lingual one would add instrumental segments, if not perceptual ones.

When some percussor causes sound vibrations with a static chamber, that sound is considered to be a segmental center. Thus the sudden closing and opening of the lips (while a velar closure is held, in order to provide static mouth air) would give repeated segments.

When the sounds from the percussors are superimposed upon the sound of an air mechanism (as with [p], [t], [k]), it does not prove convenient to analyze them as separate segments. The moment of reinforcement of the sound of an air mechanism by a percussive may be called a *percussive transition* from one segment to the next (see pp. 91, 93–94, 104–5).

After the crests and troughs in a sequence or a large number of sequences have been marked off to show the centers of the segments, each of the segments may be classified according to the type of mechanism producing it and the articulatory modifications which are added to its air stream. Whenever two segments, whether contiguous or noncontiguous, are produced by the same articulatory method and are acoustically the same, they are the same *phonetic unit,* or *phone.* An *instrumental phone* is a phone identified or identifiable by some instrumental means; repeated contiguous or noncontiguous utterances of the same instrumental phone will (by definition) be found identical, within the range of sensitivity of some particular instrument. A *real phone* is one which the average normal ear, after training, elimination of phonemic prejudice, and so on, would identify, or be physiologically capable of identifying; in repetitions of a real phone any variation detectable only by instruments is below the threshold of perceptual ability of the ear. A *perceptual phone* is one which a particular ear at a particular time believes it identifies; repeated utterances which are to a particular observer occurrences of the same perceptual phone, may to someone else be different perceptual phones; and even to the same observer at a different time (especially after phonetic training) they may " sound different," that is, be different perceptual phones for him also.

The perceptual phones of the phonetic layman always contain many more real and instrumental phones than the perceptual phones of the trained individual. A set of real phones might line up into more than one set of perceptual phones in different phonetic contexts. Before training, a speaker of English is likely not to notice varieties of his [k] phoneme; simply because they are members of a phoneme they would tend to be members of a perceptual phone. After phonetic training he may learn to recognize differences due to position of the closure relatively far front or back in the mouth, and so on, and real phones then become different perceptual phones. The problem of identifying members of phones is largely one of comparing the acoustic quality of sounds and the articulatory method of their production. This is not true of segmentation, which ignores quality as such and is concerned only with the fact that the quality has changed because of structural movements.

Perceptual and real segments in a specific continuum overlap so as to be almost identical; perceptual and real phones in the same continuum overlap much less. Languages agree very well on the places at which segmentation shall occur (except for the fluctuant points; see p. 46), but they have an infinite variety of phones of minute qualitative differences. Probably instrumental segments would be found not to differ very strikingly from real segments; one might almost say that instrumental phones for a very fine instrument must consist of unique members (since no two sounds tend to be exactly alike); they therefore differ markedly from real phones and tremendously from perceptual ones, since the latter are composed of many instrumentally different members. One can speak of a natural segmentation, since the breaks seem to be quite similar in all languages, but one may not speak of a natural choice of phones for languages, since languages employ a great variety.

A *speech sound* is, generally speaking, that part of an utterance abstracted from speech which consists of no less than one segment and no more segments (rarely more than two, perhaps never more than four or even three) than may be combined into single phonemes.

Any part of a continuum, chosen for articulatory analysis, which contains less than a segment is a *phonetic fraction* (see p. 52). These fractions may be described according to their productive mechanisms, but they lack a place in the functioning units of sounds in speech.

A *sound* may be either a speech sound, a phone, or a phonetic fraction; the term is ambiguous but convenient.

A *syllable* is a single unit of movement of the lung initiator (but for syllables from other initiators see p. 118) which includes but one crest of speed (cf. p. 108). Every occurrence of an initiator time bulge (see pp. 111–13 and Fig. 12, p. 112) followed by renewed speed of the initiator movement is a trough or border between two syllables. Physiologically, syllables may also be called chest pulses (see pp. 53–54). Instruments detecting these units locate *instrumental syllables*. *Real syllables* are those which the ear is physiologically capable of distinguishing. *Perceptual syllables* are those which an investigator actually notices at some particular time.

The segment during which the speed of the initiator movement is the greatest in the syllable is the *syllabic;* a few exceptions (e.g. in [ha]) seem to be due to an acoustic subcriterion of prominence (see p. 118). All other segments in the syllable are *nonsyllabics.* The syllabic may be considered the functional center, nucleus, or *crest* of the syllable. It is not always possible to determine where the trough of initiating movement which separates two syllables occurs; should the trough fall within a long contoid or vocoid, the sound is composed of two segments.

Syllable units and segment units are somewhat interdependent. Every close stricture within a continuum tends to prevent the egress of the air stream initiated by the pulmonic movement, and air pressure is built up behind these complete or partial strictures. The pressure accumulated in this way tends to slow down the movement of the initiator or to stop it entirely. When the strictures are released the pressure is lessened, and the speed of the initiator movement increases. These alternations of initiator movement constitute the syllable pulse. The movement of the initiator can also be slowed down by its own sets of muscles, rather than by the resistance of air pressure; this type of time-bulge alternation fuses into a single system with that produced because of changes in the air pressure. The majority of syllables are caused by changes of structural interference with the air stream and initiator movement; but, on the other hand, the strictures by themselves could give rise to very little sound (except for the percussives) if the initiator sent no air stream to cause vibrations at those points.

Strictures can be produced in isolation with a single movement of the initiator and without syllable pulsations. For example, an [s] can be made and continued with no perceptible syllable divisions within it. On the other hand, syllable pulsations can be produced in an isolated sound, e.g. [a], without the aid of structural changes. The systems of articulation and syllable movement can therefore be operated somewhat independently. For this reason also they can be operated simultaneously, superimposing their features one upon another. The description of the articulatory and acoustic characteristics of a phone must therefore be given without reference to its place in any syllable, since its syllable characteristics are subject to change depending upon the particular kind of syllable it happens to be in, and upon whether or not the phone functions as a syllabic. Its syllable function can later be stated independently as something superimposed upon its innate articulatory characteristics.

The articulatory features of the syllable are of course reflected in acoustic quality and in the articulatory nature of the syllabic. Since the trough of the syllable division tends to come at the region of heaviest air pressure, which is in turn partly conditioned by the degree to which strictures close off the air stream, segments which have the higher degrees of stricture and interrupt the air stream the most tend to be nonsyllabic; the nonsyllabic group, therefore, includes stops and fricatives more often than vocoids, although voiceless vocoids are frequent exceptions. Since sonority is to some extent conditioned by the size of the air chamber and by the lack of interference with the air stream, the contoid group also tends to be less sonorous than do the syllabics. Loudness is conditioned by the degree and type of interfering stricture within the structure of the segment and by the speed and pressure of the initiator; both of these factors tend to make syllabics louder than nonsyllabics. If sounds are uttered very rapidly together the ear tends to hear fewer perceptual syllables, since it cannot pick up the changes in the speed of the initiator movement even though they may be there; if sounds are given more slowly, and the duration of the retention of their strictures is increased, the ear is better able to pick up the changes in the initiator movement, and therefore more perceptual syllables are acoustically recorded. Features of loudness, sonority, and duration tend to make segments prominent; since syllabics generally have these features, *prominence* is likely to be the major acoustic characteristic of a syllabic. In phonetic analysis, therefore, one legitimately interprets alternations of prominence in terms of alternations of perceptual syllables.

So far in this discussion the only initiator which has been considered in syllable division has been the pulmonic one. If, however, sequences of sounds are made with any other initiator without the admixture of sounds produced from a pulmonic air stream, the syllabic sequences are produced by alternations of pulsations of that initiator. If, for example, the breath is held (to insure the quiescence of the pulmonic initiator) and a series of sounds is made with pharynx air, a sequence of syllables will be noted which are conditioned by the pulse of the laryngeal movement.

Whenever sounds produced from nonpulmonic initiators are included in a continuum which has sounds with lung air, the syllable pulse is given only by the pulmonic initiator, whereas the segments from the other initiators merely produce crests and troughs of stricture for the pulmonic sequence. A glottalized [t], for example, acts like any other type of [t] in syllable alternation if it is surrounded by lung-air vocoids.

A syllable is *checked* (or *closed*) whenever it ends in a contoid, but especially when the initiator movement is slowed down because of pressure of the air stream built up by resistance at an *arresting* segment or at groups of arresting segments functioning together. A syllable is *free* (or *open*) when it ends in a vocoid. The word ' hast ' is a syllable checked by the arresting group [st]. The word ' spa ' is a free syllable. A *trigger segment* (or group of segments acting as a whole) is one during which pressure is building up behind the strictures following a syllable trough and just before a syllable crest, in preparation for the latter; upon release of the segment the initiator movement speeds up because of the smaller degree of resisting pressure during the syllabic. The initial contoids in the following words are trigger segments: ' buy,' ' sell,' ' steal.' The medial contoids in the following words are trigger segments: ' receive,' ' pronoun.'

A *stress group* is a sequence of several syllables one of which, the *stressed syllable*, has a much stronger initiator pressure than do the others. This is not the simple result of pressure built up behind trigger segments. The location of the stressed syllable within the stress group is not determined by any articulatory features (and for that reason may be determined by the pattern of a particular linguistic system).

The smallest natural units of sound in a phonetic continuum are the segments; these are determined mostly by sequences of structural movement. A larger unit of sound is the syllable, which is partly determined by the nature of the segment strictures and partly free in that the initiator itself may make time bulges by its movement. The largest unit is the stress group, whose size phonetically is almost

completely free from determination by the segment strictures. For
each type of unit the centers tend to be definitely marked, but the
borders tend to be vague.

ARTICULATION

ARTICULATORS

At the time in the production of some sound when any moveable
part of the vocal apparatus causes any *stricture* (the partial or complete closure of an air passage) it becomes an *articulator* unless it is a

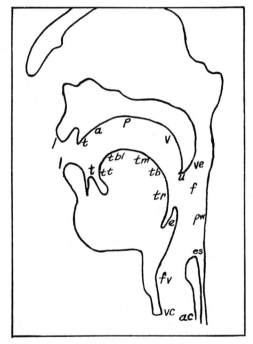

FIG. 13.   Potential articulators and points of articulation

Reading from left to right along the top of the mouth: *l*, lips; *t*, teeth; *a*, alveolar
    arch; *p*, palate; *v*, velum; *u* uvula; reading from left to right along the
    bottom of the mouth: *l*, lips, *t*, teeth; *tt*, tongue tip; *tbl*, tongue blade; *tm*,
    tongue middle; *tb*, tongue back; *tr*, tongue root; *e*, epiglottis; reading from
    top to bottom in the nasal and pharyngeal cavities: *ve*, velic; *f*, faucal pillars;
    es, esophagus; *fv*, false vocal cords; *vc*, vocal cords; *ac*, arytenoid cartilages
NOTE — *f*, *fv*, *vc*, and *ac* are not visible in the diagram. For a diagram of the
    vocal cords see Passy, *The Sounds of the French Language*, facing page 7.

closure performing the function of an initiator. All moveable parts of the vocal apparatus are *potential articulators,* since they may become active ones by fulfilling the conditions just mentioned. Potential articulators comprise the *lips* (separate or together), the lower *jaw* (either in the approximation of the lower to the upper *teeth* or in making smaller the oral cavity by closing the mouth), the *tongue* (which is divided into several articulators, since various parts may cause strictures separately; *tip, blade, middle, back,* and *root* are convenient arbitrary points of reference for these positions), the *velum,* the *uvula,* the *velic* (see p. 58), the *faucal pillars* (including with their articulation certain other factors yet unanalyzed, such as a type of lower pharyngeal constriction, glottal tension, and usually a raising of the larynx), the *epiglottis,* the *pharynx* (the root of the tongue moving backward toward some part of the pharyngeal wall, or the sides of the passage contracting, or both operations taking place at once), the *vocal cords* (sometimes known more graphically as " vocal folds "), the *arytenoid cartilages,* and the *esophageal wall* at its opening into the pharynx; the walls of the lungs and the esophagus or stomach act as initiators but not articulators. The *false vocal cords* may be potential articulators; at the present time, however, the writer has not gained any perceptual mastery over them. Presumably they act concomitantly with pharyngeal movement of some type, and are grouped with such movement by the imitation-label technic. This is largely true of movement of the epiglottis also.

Most of these items are described in practically every phonetic book, so that no elaborate descriptive statement is needed here. For a diagram labeling these articulators see Figure 13.

(see p. 58)

SHAPES OF ARTICULATORS

A cross section of an articulator from one side to the other may show that for a particular sound it is relatively *flat,* as for an interdental fricative [θ]; *grooved,* as for a sibilant, [s]; *rounded,* when both upper and lower articulators are grooved to make a relatively round aperture; *convex; contracted,* for one type of [r] which is not retroflexed; *expanded,* as for an [i] in which the sides of the tongue push out slightly between the teeth.

From front to back an articulator may be *straight; cupped* (though it is generally more convenient to consider the front and back parts of the tongue to be separate articulators when cupped, as for a velarized [t]); *retroflexed* (used only for the tongue; the tip is raised, as for a domal [n]); *humped*, as for [i]; *retracted,* as for a pharyngeal stop; *protruded,* as for interdental [t]; *central,* with front escape of air, as for [s]; *lateral,* with side escape of air, as for [l].

An articulator may combine shape from side to side with shape from front to back. Thus in an interdental [s] the tongue is protruded and grooved, in contrast with the same articulator in interdental [θ], where it is protruded and flat, or in contrast to an interdental labial (lower lip between the two sets of teeth, not just against the upper ones), where a different articulator is used, one whose shape is retracted and flat. Any part of the wall of an air chamber, whether initiator, percussor, or articulator, which is elsewhere than in a perpendicular line to its *normal* position at rest, is *displaced;* this includes all protruded ,or retracted articulators. When one articulator is displaced it may involve the displacement of a second, and prevent its normal functioning. When the tongue root, for example, is articulating near or against the back pharyngeal wall, normal front vocoidal positions cannot be taken by the front of the tongue.

In addition to the shapes already mentioned there can be made various types of distortion of some articulator which may produce slightly different nonspeech sounds. One of these is the tongue twisted lengthwise so that the tip is upside down, for an interdental stop.

POINTS OF ARTICULATION

Any section of the wall of an air chamber which is accessible to the contact or near contact of potential articulators is a potential *point* (or *region*) *of articulation,* and becomes an active one when any stricture is made at that point. Certain points of articulation are stationary parts of the vocal mechanism: *teeth, alveolar arch* (which might with more justice be called the *gingival* one, since the contact is made against the gum, not the bone; the more traditional term is retained here for convenience, and applies to the upper gum only), and *palate* (used here for the hard palate only, not the soft palate, which is labeled " velum "). See Figure 13.

When two articulators together make contract or partial stricture, this also is called a point of articulation. The two lips working together, the two vocal cords in joint operation, the back part of the tongue in conjunction with the velum, and the like, are points of articulation.

If there were no displaced articulators every articulator would have one, and only one, point of articulation. A few terms would then serve to describe all the combinations. A number of labels are conveniently used under the assumption of a normal position for an articulator in its normal point of articulation. These combinations are: *bilabial* (both lips), *alveolar* (tongue tip and gum), *palatal* (tongue middle and hard palate), *velar* (tongue back and velum), *uvular* (uvula and tongue back), *velic* (velic and wall of nasopharynx), *pharyngeal* (pharyngeal wall and tongue root), *faucal* (faucal pillars), *epiglottal* (epiglottis and pharyngeal wall), *glottal* (both vocal cords), and *esophageal* (wall of the orifice of the esophagus and wall of the pharynx). Terms might be given which show the dual nature of such articulation. If the articulator furnishes the first item, the point of articulation the second, some of those terms could be " labiolabial," " linguoalveolar," " linguovelar," " epiglottopharyngeal," " glottoglottal," and so on. This hardly seems necessary, provided the assumptions are clearly stated which affect the labels first presented.

When articulators are displaced, some new way must be found to name their relation to a point of articulation. The type of dual label suggested but discarded for the group above is conveniently used for the displaced set: the *labiodental* position (lower lip, upper teeth) is an example. Terms like " labiovelar " do not mean an articulator plus a point of articulation, but indicate a velar sound with labial modification; in the terminology for this study that sound would be called a " labialized velar " in order to avoid the difficulty.

Such double terms could well be extended to other sounds. Traditional terminology, however, tends to use labels which assume the proper relationship of articulator and point of articulation without stating both. For this reason an *interdental* sound is one in which the tip of the tongue is placed between the upper and lower teeth (not a sound made by both sets of teeth touching one another without lingual influence); a *dental* sound is one in which the tongue tip touches the backs of the teeth, usually the upper ones; a *domal* sound (i.e. *cerebral*, or *cacuminal*) implies that the tongue tip articulates somewhere behind the alveolar arch; a *retroflex* sound (the term is used more or less synonymously with "domal") is like a domal sound except that vocoids are modified by retroflexion, not by domal articulation.

This list does not exhaust the possible points of articulation or their relation to possible articulators. Theoretically a section on the hard palate or the velum, or the like, could be divided up into an infinite number of points at which an infinite number of parts of the tongue could in turn produce an unlimited number of sounds. Granting that to be true, the total number must then be reduced to a relatively small group because of the perceptual factor. An untrained person could identify only a few of these sounds if they were uttered a short time apart; if they were given one right after the other, he could distinguish many more, but still a very limited number. For this reason it cannot be acceptable phonetic procedure to act as if the number were infinite. Much preferable is actual phonetic practice, which arbitrarily fixes a few norms for points of articulation and handles any perceptible deviation from those norms in terms of departures from them.

The choice of particular points on the velum and palate as norms for the place of production of sound types is highly arbitrary, since these points and others which might have been chosen give sounds which have similar productive mechanisms and acoustic properties. The choice of norms is not so arbitrary when it establishes divisions between sounds made with the lips, the tip of the tongue, and the middle of the tongue. Sounds made with the lips are productively and acoustically quite different from types made with the tip of the tongue in normal position, and both are different from types made with the middle of the tongue, or the glottis, and so on (although just at the border between them they may shade into one another). For this reason the traditional grouping of stops into types of [p], [t], [k] is quite justifiable.

TYPES OF ARTICULATION

Normal articulation is that employed for the vast majority of sounds (e.g. [i], [s], [p]); in it an articulator approaches its point of articulation and, having reached a certain stage of stricture, may maintain that position for a longer or a shorter period of time before releasing.

In *flap articulation* the articulator gives one rapid tap against its

articulating region and then immediately releases; approach and release together are formed by a single ballistic movement. A flap
differs from normal articulation in that the stricture cannot be retained
longer than is necessary for the quick flipping contact. Acoustically
the percussive is very prominent in comparison with the air stream.
Most flaps completely close the passageway of some cavity. Samples
of flap articulation can be seen in the central contoids of American
English ' matter,' or Spanish *pero,* ' but.' Laterals may have the
central contact given and released as a quick flap. One hears but
rarely of any flaps except those with the tongue tip articulating against
the alveolar arch, but others with the same type of quick percussive
effect are possible. A labioalveolar flap in which the lower lip taps
against the upper gum is one of these.

Iterative articulation is formed by the repeated, rapid, and automatic approach and release of some stricture. Three general types
can be mentioned: *chatters, trills,* and *vibratory trills.*

Chatters are the repeated rapid partial formation of a stricture;
at their segment crests they do not completely close the air passage.
When the teeth chatter, for instance, they may make contact and
cause percussive sounds, but they do not prevent a continuous simultaneous egressive or ingressive air stream which escapes through
their interstices, even during the contact of their biting surfaces, and
causes a fricative chatter. The jaw may flutter rapidly up and down,
causing neither dental contact nor fricative partial stricture, and
produce chattered vocoids. The abdominal muscles may give rapid
pulsations and cause *syllabically chattered continuants* of any type
within the oral, nasal, and pharyngeal cavities (note some types of
laughter).

Trills are iterative strictures of a kind which completely close the
air passage within which they occur; within a trill the separate pulsations or contacts are audible. Trills may be considered automatic
repetitions of flap articulation. They may be made by the lips, cheek,
tongue tip (as in Spanish), side of the tongue (these lateral trills are
usually quite fricative), uvula (as in the commoner pronunciation of
French or German), velic (in a snore; usually with ingressive lung
air through both oral and nasal cavities), esophageal opening (in belch
sounds; often the separate pulsations are not clearly audible, so that
the trill approaches the vibratory type), and vocal cords (trills so

made are often heard in the speech of people who are talking in a tone of voice very low as compared with normal style; in this case the glottal trill is substituted for voice; children often make the sound for self-amusement; the attainment of the sound made by " singing two notes lower than you can " tends to give one pitch of the trill). Sounds which I had for some time been tentatively suggesting were epiglottal trills have proved to be pharyngeal, since while making the sounds one can touch with his finger the stationary tip of the epiglottis (I am indebted to Dr. Fritz Frauchiger, of the University of Oklahoma, for aid in this discovery); a view through a dentist's mirror shows the pharynx immediately above the epiglottis contracted to the size of a lead pencil, while the soft walls of the pharynx at that point are flapping, with saliva completing the closure perhaps somewhat as water is used in a gargle.

Vibratory trills automatically, repeatedly, and completely close an air passage, but the separate percussive sounds are never clearly audible, and usually are not audible at all. Such trills may be produced at the lips most easily if a small passageway is provided by continued firm contact at one or both sides of the lips; a mechanism related to this seems to be the type used by players of brass instruments (for example, a cornet) to initiate the sound vibrations of *lip* " *voice* " which enter the metal resonators. In a similar way, *voice* is a vibratory trill produced by the vocal cords and modified by pharyngeal, nasal, and oral mechanisms.

The exact relation between trills and vibratory trills cannot be analyzed by the auditory articulation technic since the ear cannot catch the separate factors in vibration. One interesting analogy can be mentioned; if a stick is drawn slowly along a picket fence, the separate percussions are obvious; if the stick is drawn very rapidly, the percussions tend to merge into a steady tone.

This analogy will not explain the relationship between voice and *trillization* (glottal trill modified by pharyngeal, nasal, and oral cavities). The second cannot be simply a slow form of the first. The following data apply to the sounds as made by the writer, but may have to be modified for other speakers.

If voice is produced with some accompanying oral formation and then the sound is whispered or breathed with as little change of glottal position as possible apart from the unvoicing, a markedly different kind of whisper is attained in comparison with that which results from the same procedure if one starts with trillization, which cuts off a large percentage of the escaping air. This parallels the fact that an alveolar sibilant [z] with voice is plainly heard, but the same oral formation with trillization results in little or no sibilant (unless the stricture is made smaller) because of the weak air stream. Kinesthetically, the author judges that in passing from voice to trillization the posterior section of the glottis is closed; in passing from trillization to voice a relaxation takes place which allows the posterior section to vibrate, rather than the anterior section only. This statement has not been checked satisfactorily with instrumental research by the author, and quite probably will be subject to modification.

Another major evidence that trillization is not slow voice is given by permitted pitches. If glottal trill were slow voice analogous to the slow movement of a stick on a picket fence, then the highest pitch of trillization would be lower than the lowest pitch of voice. This is not the case. The pitches of both types can be controlled separately; trillization can be given in both low and high pitches, in approximately the same range as voice (possibly voice tends to be a trifle higher than the analogous position for trillization); one can sing up and down the scale in either. If one starts with a glottal trill, the addition of more tension and a more powerful air stream does not raise the pitch of the trill to turn it into voice, but tends simply to shut off the glottis completely and stop all sound; a glottal trill which starts with very strong lung pressure and tension must have definite relaxation (rather than further tension) of the vocal cords before they can produce voice.

If the two formations were identical except for the speed of the vocal-cord movement, they could not be combined into a new composite type. *Laryngealization* may conveniently be said to be trillization with superimposed voice. Knowledge of the precise method of production must await instrumental analysis. In these sounds the separate percussions of the glottal trill are audible while at the same time regular voice vibrations add their characteristic sound. The combination can be sung up and down the scale. In English one often hears laryngealized vowels. If a person speaks in a low tone of voice, and the voicing tends to be obscured or turned into a " rumble " or " growl," two stages of this change can be heard. The first is that in which voice is preserved but separate percussions from glottal trill begin to be heard more or less dimly, or even strongly. In the second stage the normal voice vibrations are completely eliminated, and only trillization remains. The sequence of vocoids and contoids remains the same, since vocoidal quality is more the product of the oral resonators than of the vocal-cord movement. In this respect trillized or laryngealized speech parallels whispered speech except that a different type of substitution is made for voice in the vocoids and voiced contoids.

A certain type of vibration of the vocal cords is known as *falsetto* (i.e. *false voice*). In this formation a certain " set " is given to the glottis which may be carried through other sound types — not just the vibratory trill. This characteristic is not subject to auditory articulation analysis, but certainly includes some type of reduced aperture and consequent diminished air stream; when sibilants are uttered with the vocal cords in position for falsetto, they are reduced in audibility just as they are when trillized. Passing from voice to false voice, and vice versa, provides the basis for *yodeling*. Most women seem incapable of using false voice; the author has recently observed a girl of fifteen months use a type of yodeling, while crying, where high screams appeared to be in false voice and the " break " to voice seemed to be clearly audible. Some women can " squeal " or scream in false voice.

False whisper is a whisper produced when the cords are in position for false voice but are not vibrating. Such a whisper is quite sharp and high-pitched, but not so high or sharp as a whisper which has voice position of the vocal cords and simultaneous faucal constriction. *False trillization* is a glottal trill produced from falsetto position. *False laryngealization* is a combination of false trillization and false voice. False voice, false laryngealization, and false trillization can all be sung up and down the scale with the same pitch and qualitative characteristics that falsetto has in relation to voice on the one hand and that trillization and laryngealization have to voice on the other.

Fortis articulation entails strong, tense movements within the types of articulation already described but relative to a norm assumed for all sounds; this norm cannot be delineated, but is a convenient fiction as a basis for comparison. Weak articulation is *lenis*. Fortis movement of an initiator tends to make relatively loud sounds, and brings acoustic judgments to bear on the fortis nature of sounds. To a large extent in general practice the term " fortis " is a term of contextual function, indicating that one sound is louder than another contiguous to it. In order to separate usage in regard to articulatory, acoustic, and contextual data, this study will use " fortis " and " lenis " of articulation only; " loud " and " soft " of acoustic judgments as regards an assumed norm of loudness; " contextually loud " to show acoustic judgments of the relation of one sound to another in context. Thus the hissing of English [s] is loud, but not fortis, in comparison with [z]; the lingual strictures seem to be the same (hence neither fortis nor lenis), but the noise of the hissing of the [s] is louder because it has a stronger air stream at the lingual stricture (the partial glottal closure for voicing reduces the strength of the air stream for [z]).

Spasmodic articulation is a type produced by sudden movements beyond the control of the individual. Sounds employing this articulatory device include the cough, sneeze, hiccough, and frequently laughter, or belching. Even if the phonetician can voluntarily simulate these sounds, they are apt to fall short of the genuine spasmodic production. Trills have an automatic repetitive element, but their initiation is not spasmodic.

STRICTURE

FUNCTION OF STRICTURES

In Chapter IV, differences were noted in the action of various kinds of strictures and of the various cavities. They have distinct places in the economy of sound production. In this section a working statement is given to facilitate description of these differences.

When the closure (or, more rarely, the near closure) of a passageway allows that moving section of the wall of the air chamber to be an initiator, the closure is an *initiating stricture*. The closed glottis is an initiating stricture during implosives and glottalized sounds. Velar closure is of the initiating type during clicks and egressive clicks.

When two cavities provide potential egress to an air stream, but one of the passageways is closed by a complete stricture, so that the air is shunted out the other cavity, that closure is a *valvate stricture* or *valvate articulator*. Such closures act like valves; in a pipe organ the bellows would correspond to an initiator, and the mouth of a pipe to an articulator; but a valve which opens to allow air to reach a pipe while not altering the sound as such would be roughly analogous to a valvate stricture. In all oral sounds with lung air the closed velic prevents air escaping through the nose; only this valvate stricture makes [s], [f], [z], [i] into purely oral sounds. During nasalized oral sounds there is no valvate stricture, and therefore air escapes through both the nose and the mouth. For the production of nasals a valvate stricture must be present in the oral cavity; the choice of the point at which this closure occurs makes the difference between [m] and [n].

The closure of the entrance into the esophagus is related to valvate strictures, but differs in several respects. Its normal position is that of closure, with no compressed or rarefied air stream in the esophageal cavity. Further, even were the entrance to the cavity open, no egress would be provided for the air stream. Closures which shut off such an egressless cavity are *subvalvate*. During (voiceless) pharynx-air sounds the closed glottis serves simultaneously in initiating and subvalvate functions. During belches which have no voicing from a simultaneous stream of lung air the glottal closure is subvalvate but not initiating.

In reference to the other cavities the oral cavity may be classed as *primary*, the nasal one as *secondary*, and the pharyngeal cavity as *tertiary*. The pulmonic and esophageal cavities need not be given rank in this system since their function is restricted to that of initiators except for sounds which under normal conditions are below the perceptual level (e.g. the sound of air within the alveoli of the lungs; medical men use a stethoscope to listen to these sounds).

Various reasons can be presented for the convenience of this ranking. A great variety of strictures can be made in the oral cavity since the tongue is extremely flexible and can make contact at many different points; in the nasal cavity only a few different strictures can be made (at the velic; the nostrils have little or no audible effect on sound when they are moved), and the kinesthetic sense of their presence is weak; strictures in the pharynx tend to group themselves into a very few kinesthetically recognized types or under imitation labels because of the lack of such sensation. The individual oral variations therefore tend to become prominent, while the others are readily described as modifications of these detailed types. Oral sounds can be produced by oral mechanisms acting by themselves, but all pharyngeal sounds are in some way modified by the oral or nasal cavities (the continuants, by the air passing through such cavities; the voiced stops, by induction mechanisms). Oral quality is more basic than pharyngeal quality in that vowel type or timbre persists despite various glottalic or pharyngeal formations; were pharyngeal and oral strictures treated as of equal function, voiceless and voiced [u] would have to be placed in basically different categories instead of being considered varieties of the same vocoid, with its form modified by voicing. Strictures of equal type, degree, and function, except for their placement in different cavities, can in this way be separated according to their decidedly different usages (e.g. fricative partial strictures at the lips, at the velic, and at the glottis do not affect total sound production in analogous ways; this contrast is due to difference in cavity function). During a [u], friction at the glottis would leave the sound a vocoid, but labial friction would change it into a contoid.

Primary strictures include all articulating strictures within the oral cavity. In an alveolar click stop, for example, the velar closure is not primary, since it is an initiator, not an articulator; the alveolar closure is primary.

Primary strictures do not all function alike and need to be divided into several groups. A *primary valvate stricture* is an oral valvate closure during nasal sounds (e.g. the alveolar closure for [n]).

When two or more oral strictures are present which are neither valvate nor initiating, there may still be differences of function between them. In a labialized sibilant the labial stricture is subordinate to the alveolar one; in a palatalized labial stop the palatal stricture is subordinate to the labial one. When two oral strictures occur, the one which has the closest position, which approaches nearest the state of closure, is *primary* and the other *subprimary;* three degrees of stricture are usually sufficient to classify this differentiation: (1) a closure; (2) a stricture producing audible local friction; (3) a stricture with inaudible friction or cavity friction only. Thus the labialization of [s] was subprimary, since it was frictionless as contrasted with the primary fricative stricture at the alveolar arch; the palatalization of [p] was subprimary whereas the labial closure was primary, since the first had frictionless position whereas the second had closure.

If within the oral cavity two strictures occur which are neither valvate nor initiating and which are of the same degree of closure, they cause a *double* primary stricture (or a double subprimary stricture if some other noninitiating stricture is of a higher degree of closure in the cavity). The most common type of double primary stricture is that of a high but rounded vocoid (e.g. [u], which has frictionless labial and velar strictures). One can also make a fricative double primary stricture with fricative strictures at the same velar and labial points of articulation; in this case the velar stricture has to be of a close variety or else its sound will be masked out and made inaudible by the vibrations at the lips. Lung-air stops with closures at the velum and the lips (plus a valvate closure at the velic) might be described as having double primary strictures, but if the front closure releases first it becomes a percussor for an oral static mechanism which is present simultaneously with a pulmonic air mechanism whose primary stricture is the velar closure.

Secondary strictures are produced in the nasal cavity. A partial velic stricture which gives harsh friction at that point is a secondary stricture, as is the cavity friction of nasal resonance during nasalized sounds.

Cavity differences separate the secondary function of velic closure from that of primary oral closure in stops like [o], [b], [k], even in sequences such as [mbm], [ntn]. In fact, it is convenient upon the basis of this difference in stops, and the valvate function of velic closure in oral spirants, to state that a velic closure is always valvate. Descriptively, then, for stops the velic " first " closes off the nasal cavity, and " then " the oral closure arrests the air stream; the actual order does not always conform to this in groups like [mbm]. Our normal writing of stops in such a sequence by means of a letter emphasizing the position of the oral closure ([p] in contrast to [t], bilabial in contrast to alveolar articulation) reflects the basic assumption of this functional difference, with the oral stricture primary.

Undesirable alternatives to this descriptive order in stops are to consider the velic and oral closures of equal rank (in which case there would be no explanation for their functional differences), or the approaching closure primary (which would force the interpretation of the second segment in [nt] as a " velic stop "), or the release primary (which would force the first segment in [dn] to be a " velic stop," and would prevent the analysis of unreleased final stops). If either the approach or the release is to be considered essential to the analysis of a stop, then one of the goals laid down for this investigation could never be attained — a system which allows the description of a phonetic fraction at any point in a sequence — since under these conditions the center of a stop could never be analyzed by itself.

Basic classification of nasals ([m], [n], and the like) is usually done by means of the position of their oral closures. This differentiation is emphasized by the primary position of their valvate strictures, while their nature in its broadest features is determined by the cavity friction of the passageway in the direct line of the air stream, that is, the nasal cavity (cf. escape cavity, p. 140).

Tertiary strictures are those within the pharyngeal cavity. They include all types of glottal modification and strictures made by the wall of the pharyngeal cavity, the epiglottis, faucal pillars, and so on.

The only strictures which are pertinent to the description of any phonetic fraction are those which exist within the active air chamber for that sound. A glottal stop, for example, has one tertiary stricture, the glottal closure, but has no secondary or primary strictures. The stop [k] has a secondary velic valvate stricture, a subvalvate esophageal stricture (which can usually be assumed to exist without specific mention of it), and a primary velar closure; labialization would not be subprimary to the sound since the lips are not within the active chamber (which includes only the pharyngeal and pulmonic cavities and that section of the oral cavity which is behind the velar closure).

The *acme stricture* of any sound is the highest ranking one within the active chamber. With glottal stop the acme stricture is the tertiary glottal closure, since neither secondary nor primary strictures are present within the active chamber (which includes only the pulmonic cavity and that lower edge of the pharyngeal cavity which the glottis itself constitutes). With [k] the acme stricture is the primary velar closure. With labialized [s] the primary alveolar stricture, not the subprimary labial one, is the acme stricture. The acme stricture, therefore, is the articulator with the nearest approach to closure within the highest ranking cavity of the active air chamber.

All noninitiating, nonvalvate, nonacme strictures are *qualifiers,* unless, as in nasals, the acme stricture is itself a valvate closure. No stricture may be considered to qualify a valvate closure even if it possesses higher rank; nasal resonance in nasals does not merely qualify the oral closure but, rather, is basically and essentially characteristic of the resultant sound type. Qualifiers modify the effect produced by the acme stricture itself. Thus labialization may qualify an [s], voicing may qualify a labial stop, nasalization may qualify a vocoid. In the descriptive order one first locates the active air chamber and then labels the initiating, valvate, and acme strictures (although the last two may sometimes coincide; e.g. in [n] the oral closure is the acme stricture, but valvate); all other strictures (except for the secondary cavity in nasals) are qualifiers, whether tertiary, secondary, or subprimary.

Whenever any sound is qualified by cavity friction from a stricture of lower rank than the acme one, whether or not the stricture is in the same cavity (e.g. subprimary), it has been *modified*. Such modification by the lips is *labialization;* by the middle of the tongue approximating the palate, *palatalization;* by the back of the tongue at the velum, *velarization;* these are subprimary types of qualification. *Nasalization* causes the secondary modification of sounds by adding nasal resonance to them. Tertiary modification includes qualification induced by the approximation of the faucal pillars (and other phenomena in the pharynx not subject to observation in a hand mirror), *faucalization,* or by the approximation of the wall of the pharynx to the root of the tongue, *pharyngealization.*

The frictionless iteratives may also be modifiers. The initial stages of a glottalized bilabial stop, for example, may have the modification of an alveolar trill. The most frequent modification of related type is glottal vibratory trill applied to any lung-air sound (except glottal stop) to make it voiced. Trillization and laryngealization may likewise modify the same types of sounds, but with a different resultant acoustic quality.

Whenever the acme stricture of any continuant or stop is qualified by a stricture of lower rank which gives local friction (see pp. 71–72, 138–39), the sound has been *frictionalized.* Thus nasals, frictionless laterals, or vocoids may be frictionalized by glottal stricture during whisper, or by any other local friction in the pharyngeal cavity.

It becomes difficult to frictionalize sounds with outer primary local friction since the inner friction tends to be masked out by the outer type; simultaneous inner and outer friction can be produced (e.g. glottal friction as for a whisper during [s]), but in order to be heard the inner stricture must usually be closer than would be necessary if it were qualifying a vocoid.

Stops may be temporarily frictionalized by the movement of the capped air stream through some partial stricture before the final equalization of pressure. A bilabial voiceless stop, for example, may have at its commencement the weakly added sound of air pushing past a close partial stricture of the tongue at the velum. Stops may also be frictionalized by whisper, and so on.

The fricative iteratives may qualify sounds. Vocoids which are frictionalized by a fricative glottal vibratory trill are timbres of " voiced [h]."

The trills can themselves be qualified. An alveolar trill, for example, may have velar friction added. The trills can also be modified by labialization and similar processes. The most common qualification of a trill, as well as of any other sound type, is by a tertiary vibratory trill, voice. Voice can be added even to a triple primary trill wherein the lips, tongue tip, and uvula are all trilling simultaneously.

When strictures are present during some sound but lie in a passive chamber rather than the active one they are *passive primary, passive secondary,* or *passive tertiary* types. In [k] any labialization is passive primary, as are palatalization and the like. In describing sequences, rather than individual fractions, it is convenient to call passive strictures *semipassive* if they are due to become active in the following segment. All semipassive or passive strictures are of inferior rank to strictures within the active air chamber. In the sequence [gwa], for example, the labialization of the stop in anticipation of the following release to [w] is semipassive primary and of lower rank for the active pulmonic-pharyngeal air chamber than is the tertiary stricture at the glottis which produces the voicing.

When two or more mechanisms are used simultaneously to form a sound, each mechanism may have its own acme stricture. In a voiced alveolar click the acme stricture for the lung air is the inner side of the velar closure, while the acme stricture for the mouth air is the alveolar closure. In [g] the closure at the velum is the acme stricture; since the vibration is carried to some slight extent through that obstruction, the oral cavity becomes an induction mechanism, and, if there is rounding, the lips may act as an active primary stricture for that mechanism. This effect of the labialization is above the threshold of perception only in extraordinary circumstances (e.g. when the lips are rapidly opened and then overrounded in repeated succession, and even here the audibility is very slight indeed), so that in general this induction mechanism is not a part of a perceptual unit and can be ignored.

When a single closure has two or more simultaneous functions in which the inner side of the closure causes the strictural function for one mechanism and the outer side does so for the second, it becomes convenient to discuss the closure as a single stricture with double function rather than to describe it as articulating simultaneously at separate and unrelated inner and outer points. In the voiced nasalization of an alveolar click the acme stricture for lung air is the velar closure; the same closure functions as the initiator for the simultaneous mouth air.

During the strictures for most continuants only a part of the potential opening is used. For bilabial fricatives the sides of the lips tend to be closed; during vocoids the side of the tongue often makes some contact; with whisper the anterior part of the glottis may be closed. Contacts produced in this way for parts of potential openings are *adjuncts* to primary, secondary, or tertiary strictures. Adjuncts are not valvate, since they do not completely prevent passage of air through a cavity; they restrict the size of an opening by their contact, without completely closing off its aperture.

Side adjuncts such as the contact at the edges of the lips for [w] produce central continuants. *Center adjuncts* produce lateral continuants such as [l]. Adjuncts may occur on both sides of a passage or on a single side only; they may have contact on one side and the center of a passage for unilateral sounds.

Strictures function in two general ways. One type initiates air streams and controls the cavities through which the air stream finds egress. The other type interferes with the air stream in such a way as to cause vibrations. Functions of the second type of stricture differ principally (1) according to the cavity in which they occur and (2) according to the degree of stricture.

DEGREES OF STRICTURE

In Chapter V the problem of consonant–vowel division was discussed. Strictures do not all interfere to the same extent with the transit of air through a passageway. Differences of acoustic result in certain respects demand acoustic criteria, as was shown in that chapter. Further, as was there demonstrated, criteria for vowel–consonant delineation are so varied that the division of sounds into those two groups has not been satisfactory. The present section of Chapter VII attempts to carry the classification of sounds a step further by utilizing both acoustic criteria and criteria of degrees of stricture. Resultant from this procedure is a classification of sounds which, among other things, gives the author's answer to the vowel–consonant problem.

In relative terms not objectively fixed the extent of the region of stricture (from another point of view the size of the articulator) from front to back may be *extensive* or *restricted;* [ʃ] has a more extensive stricture (a longer groove) than does [s]. From side to side the opening may be *narrow* (limited by adjuncts) or *wide;* [2] the stricture for [o] is wider than for [u]. From top to bottom the opening may be *close* or *open;* [i] is closer than [e].

Any of these contrasted groupings can be subdivided into various arbitrary numbers of relative degrees. For close versus open stricture in vocoids investigators often find it convenient to use six: high, mid, low; close and open high, close and open mid, close and open low. Jones's " cardinal vowel " scheme [3] is perhaps the most convenient and objective classification of this type.

The shapes of articulators may be described by using these terms. A grooved tongue, for example, is narrow and open with extensive region of stricture; the deeper the groove, the opener the stricture.

A stricture may be retained for varying lengths of time: the duration may be *long* or *short* (or of other lengths described with reference to some relative, convenient standard). In pitch, especially

[2] This departs from more general usage which makes " narrow " and " close," " wide " and " open," more or less synonymous. Since two sets of contrasts need to be represented it seemed better to specialize the first terms for slightly different meanings.

[3] Jones, *An Outline of English Phonetics* [4], §§ 131–47.

in relation to a vibratory trill of the vocal cords, sounds may be *high, low,* or *mid.*

All of these differences can be measured by instruments in terms of millimeters, seconds, vibrations per second, and so on. If points of reference are established by such a measurement, then it may be stated that strictures are objectively extensive, narrow, close, long, high, and so on, in respect to these standards. Apart from such a standard, these terms are objectively vague since they are then relative to a standard which is little more than the subjective impression of a particular observer for the median usage of a particular individual. Apart from such an objective standard the terms readily become influenced by contextual factors.

Strictures may be *complete* or *partial*. The first type completely closes a passageway, so that no air can pass through it during the maintenance of the stricture. Partial strictures diminish the size of a passageway, but not so much that air cannot pass through. The oral closures in stops and nasals are complete strictures; the oral strictures in all fricatives or vowels are partial.

Partial strictures may be of a *local* or *cavity* type (see pp. 70–72). In voiced sounds local strictures produce a friction noise which can be heard above the voicing, but the cavity strictures of voiced sounds affect the resonance and quality of the sounds without giving audible friction at the specific points of their strictures. Thus the criterion for the difference is an acoustic one — presence or absence of localized friction in voiced sounds. In voiceless sounds the difference is still present, but is not so marked, and the border line is not so clear-cut; localized friction caused by air passing over a sharp edge or through a small hole contrasts with cavity friction caused by the voiceless air stream passing through a cavity (whose shape is determined in part by the stricture in question) and inciting the natural resonance of the cavity. *Local friction* tends to be nonperiodic, or noisy; *cavity friction* (especially in voiced sounds) tends to be periodic, or musical. Samples of local stricture are glottal position for whisper, the alveolar articulation in [s], [z], and the labiodental articulation in [f]; cavity stricture includes labial position for [u], velic or nasal position for [m], glottal position for voiceless vowel.

When no obvious change of the position of some part of the wall of a cavity makes a partial stricture (e.g. when in the oral cavity the tongue is in flat position of rest rather than humped for a high vocoid and the lips are open and relatively flat rather than rounded), the cavity as a whole functions as a cavity stricture. The whole nasal cavity acts in this way for nasalization of other sounds. When a partial stricture, such as high tongue position, is of the cavity type, it combines with the unchanged portion of the cavity wall so that together they act as a single unit in cavity friction.

Local friction versus cavity friction represents an acoustic difference with an acoustic criterion to draw the line of demarcation at the *friction point* between them. The identical articulatory mechanism with the identical strictures may produce in certain cases either cavity friction or local friction if the pressure of the air stream varies because of changes of the pressure of the initiator. The sound [I] with normal pressure of the air stream has only cavity friction. If the sound is made very loud, with extra lung pressure, local friction may be heard at the high front part of the tongue. If the lung pressure is very weak, no sound whatsoever will be heard. When all essential articulatory movements and all requisite strictures are present to produce a certain sound, but the pressure of the initiator is so weak that neither cavity nor local friction is above the threshold of perception, *zero sounds* of various types result (e.g. most frictionless continuants with pharynx air). Assuming a norm of pressure, a sound which would under that norm give cavity friction becomes an *accentuated* friction sound when local friction is heard because of supranormal pressure. A localized fricative which loses that friction and is heard as a sound with cavity friction because of subnormal air-stream movement is *debilitated* sound. For example, the sibilant [z] usually becomes a debilitated vocoid if trillization is substituted for voice, since the air stream which is allowed to pass through the trilling glottis is insufficient to produce audible local friction at the alveolar arch.

An air stream as a whole may be interrupted in ways analogous to that in which a single passageway is blocked. *Stops* are sounds such as [p], [t], [d], in which the air stream is completely interrupted, or capped. *Continuants* are sounds in which the air stream has some egress, as in [s], [f], [m], [o], through some partial stricture (or open cavity functioning as a cavity stricture). Stops may require one closure in order to interrupt the air stream (e.g. glottal stop or pharyngeal stop), two closures (all oral stops with lung air require valvate velic closure also), or three closures (oral stops with pharynx air add initiating glottal closure; double stops have two oral closures and velic closure, with lung air). A few stops use four closures (double stops with pharynx air; clicks with simultaneous glottalized or implosive velar stop with velic release). In addition to the closures enumerated, these sounds have a subvalvate esophageal closure; only in glottal stop, clicks, and sounds of some minor mechanisms is it not theoretically essential, but even there it is present except in the belch sounds.

Continuants are best subdivided in two ways. The two classifications used together are much more convenient than either one by itself.

1. When local friction versus cavity friction is the basic criterion, all continuants with local friction at any point are *frictionals* (e.g. [s̩], [f], whispered vocoids, fricative [l], " voiced [h] "), while all continuants with no local friction (e.g. [m], [o], [h], frictionless [l]) are *nonfrictionals* (or *frictionless* sounds, or sounds with cavity friction only).

2. The second classification of continuants utilizes a more complicated set of differentiating criteria. The first dichotomy of the second classification is made by a choice of the highest ranking *escape cavity*, that is, the cavity of highest rank through which the air stream is escaping or entering the vocal apparatus to or from the atmosphere (cf. pp. 133, 141–44). *Orals* include all continuants in which the air stream passes through the primary (i.e. oral) cavity (e.g. [f], [o], whispered [o]); orals include, also, sounds in which the air is passing at the same time through the secondary (i.e. nasal) cavity (e.g. nasalized [a]). *Nasals* comprise all sounds wherein the air escape is limited to the nasal cavity (e.g. [m], and voiceless [m] with strong local velic friction as in the rough clearing of the nose), that is, where there is a primary valvate stricture.

There can be no parallel third group of continuants with the pharynx as the highest-ranking escape cavity, since in every continuant in which the air passes through the pharynx it also passes through either the nasal or the oral cavity, both of which outrank the pharynx. If the air stream passes through the pharynx but is capped by closures at the velic and in the oral cavity, the sound is no longer a continuant but a stop (e.g. [b], [k]).

The next subdivision of this second classification of continuants is made by the criterion of the presence or absence of local friction in the highest-ranking escape cavity. In this classification, as is not true of the one which divides continuants into frictionals and non-frictionals, local friction or the lack of it is completely disregarded when it occurs in any other than the highest-ranking escape cavity. Orals with local friction in the oral cavity are *fricative orals* (e.g. [f], [s]); when without oral local friction, orals are *resonant orals* (e.g. [o], [l], whispered [a], timbres of " voiced [h] "). Nasals with local friction at the velic are *fricative nasals* (very rare, limited almost to types of rough clearing of the nose); when without velic local friction, nasals are *resonant nasals* (e.g. [m], [n]). For convenience, however, resonant nasals are called simply " nasals " elsewhere in the study unless this type of context necessitates the use of the adjectives " fricative " and " resonant " for clarity. The fricative nasals are very rare even as nonspeech sounds.

A third criterion divides orals, but not nasals. Some orals have central escape of the air in respect to the tongue or lips, whereas others have a lateral air escape. Children frequently amuse themselves by making linguolabial lateral resonant orals in which the tongue tip is placed between the lips and moved from side to side; as the tongue tip passes the median point in the lips the air stream is momentarily but completely capped. The orals comprise *central fricative orals* (e.g. [s]); *lateral fricative orals* (e.g. fricative [l]); *lateral resonant orals* (e.g. frictionless [l]); and *central resonant orals* (e.g. [o], [h]).

A diagram for comparison of the two classifications is given in Charts 1–2.

Since in the second classification the criterion of local friction is applied only to phenomena in the highest-ranking escape cavity and no reference is made to phenomena in the others, it must be carefully noted that resonant orals or resonant nasals which are without local friction in their escape cavities may yet be frictionals because of local friction elsewhere. When these same sounds were described from the viewpoint of the function of their strictures (see p. 134), they were said to be *frictionalized* vocoids, and the like, because of the

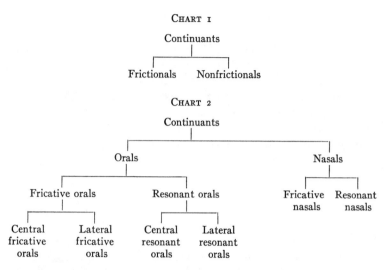

CHART 1

Continuants

Frictionals   Nonfrictionals

CHART 2

Continuants

Orals

Nasals

Fricative orals

Resonant orals

Fricative nasals   Resonant nasals

Central fricative orals

Lateral fricative orals

Central resonant orals

Lateral resonant orals

subordinate function of the frictional strictures; frictionalized vocoids are simultaneously frictionals and resonant orals. Frictionalized resonant orals include the following: whispered vocoids and whispered frictionless laterals; vocoids and frictionless laterals with voiced glottal local friction; vocoids and frictionless laterals with voiced or voiceless pharyngeal local friction; vocoids and frictionless laterals with local velic friction; and so on. Frictionalized nasals include nasals with any type of pharyngeal local friction.

Timbres of [h] (i.e. voiceless vocoids) and the average voiced vocoid (i.e. the ordinary voiced " vowel ") are both nonfrictionals, and also are both resonant orals. Whispered vocoids (i.e. the average whispered " vowel," voiceless vocoids with added glottal local friction) and timbres of " voiced [h] " (i.e. voiced vocoids with glottal local friction) are frictionals, but also are resonant orals. If one represents voiced vocoids by V, and voiceless whispered ones by W, convenient proportions may be given (cf. p. 72) to show these relationships:

$$[h] : W :: V : [ɦ] \text{ or } V : [h] :: [ɦ] : W$$

The degree of openness of strictures in sounds partly determines the frequency with which the segments appear as syllabics (cf. pp. 117–18). Instead of dividing sounds into stops and continuants, therefore, one may divide them into types which are most frequently syllabic, less frequently syllabic, and rarely or never syllabic. The contents of the groups might be determined by an elaborate frequency count in languages over the world, but the three most basic groups are readily identifiable without this procedure.

The phonetic description of these groups has to be made in terms of the same segment characteristics which have already formed the basis of previous classifications. The first classification of continuants, above, into frictionals and nonfrictionals, gives results which cannot correlate syllable features neatly, since syllabic action is conditioned not only by the degrees of stricture, but also by the rank of the cavities in which are present the different strictures. Precisely for this reason subdivisions of that classification do not serve a sufficiently useful purpose to be included here, and therefore have been omitted.

The second classification into continuants, however, takes account of the rank of cavities and can be readily used for neat descriptions of the three major groups of sounds with different syllabic frequencies.

The sounds which as a group function most frequently as syllabics are *vocoids*. Phonetically they comprise the central resonant orals as already defined. Vocoids include practically all sounds which are usually called " vowels " (whether voiced, voiceless, or whispered), except that " fricative vowels " are excluded, while " vowel glides " such as [r], [w], and [y] are included.

All nonvocoids are *contoids*. This term more closely approximates the general term " consonant " than any other used by me. Contoids include stops, fricative nasals, lateral resonant orals, and central fricative orals.

The resonant nasals and lateral resonant orals comprise a group of contoid sounds that are often syllabic, but by no means so often as the vocoids. The remaining controls (the stops, fricative orals, and fricative nasals) are rarely syllabic.

The *resonants* comprise the resonant orals (central and lateral) and resonant nasals; they have no local friction in their escape cavities (possible exceptions may be nasally frictionalized vocoids — a sound type exceedingly difficult to make, if not unutterable). They are the sound types most frequently syllabic. The *nonresonants* comprise the fricative orals (central and lateral) and stops; they impede the air stream sharply, by having local friction in an escape cavity, or by interrupting the air stream entirely. They are sound types which are rarely syllabic (but see the syllabic [s] in ' pst! ' and many other sounds as syllabics when pronounced in isolation). The *sonorants* are nonvocoid resonants and comprise the lateral resonant orals and resonant nasals (e.g. [m], [n], and [l]). The presence or absence of local friction in the pharyngeal cavity does not affect possible syllabic function, as can be seen by the use of whispered speech in which glottally frictionalized voiceless vocoids are the normal syllabics.

Chart 3 shows in diagrammatic form the three groups arranged according to syllabic frequency and according to the resonance of the escape cavities.

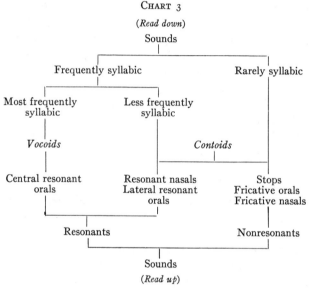

CHART 3

(*Read down*)

Sounds

Frequently syllabic   Rarely syllabic

Most frequently   Less frequently
syllabic   syllabic

Vocoids   *Contoids*

Central resonant   Resonant nasals   Stops
orals   Lateral resonant   Fricative orals
                    orals   Fricative nasals

Resonants   Nonresonants

Sounds

(*Read up*)

The phonetic groups may be realigned and additional nomenclature given them according to their function in phoneme and syllable contexts. Since phoneme structure differs from language to language, final labels must be decided upon for the functional groups of each language after its analysis by the phonemicist. Usually, however, phoneme structure is so closely related to (or conditioned by) syllable structure that, for many languages, groupings by syllable-context function is sufficient. The terms used below in regard to syllable function remain flexible and subject to change and amplification by specific phoneme function (cf. p. 78), but are nevertheless sufficiently stable to be of general value and to serve in phonetic, if not always in phonemic, descriptions.

All vocoids are simultaneously *vowels* at the time that they are functioning as syllable crests (syllabics: e.g. the vocoid segments in ' camp,' ' bit,' ' fur '). All contoids are *syllabic contoids* when they are functioning as syllable crests (e.g. the syllabics in ' pst! ' ' sh! ' ' mhm '; the second syllabic in ' bottle,' ' button '; the isolated unreleased sound [b]).

All vocoids are *nonsyllabic vocoids* while functioning as nonsyllabics (e.g. [y] in ' young '; [w] in ' woo '; [r] in ' rich '). All contoids while functioning as nonsyllabics are *consonants* (e.g. the first sounds in ' pie,' ' see,' ' life,' ' nose ').

It should be noted that the vocoid–contoid division is a dichotomous one, of all sounds, but that the vowel–consonant division is not, since vowels and consonants do not, in the definition of this study, include syllabic contoids or nonsyllabic vocoids. A possible alternate nomenclature would call all sounds " vowels " when syllabic, and all sounds " consonants " when nonsyllabic; but this would merely duplicate the terms " syllabic " and " nonsyllabic," and depart much further from current usage of the terms " vowel " and " consonant " than is at all necessary.

Charts 4 and 5 diagram the relationship between vowels and consonants.

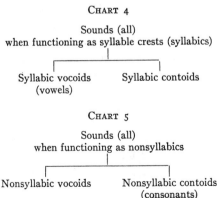

CHART 4

Sounds (all)
when functioning as syllable crests (syllabics)

Syllabic vocoids   Syllabic contoids
(vowels)

CHART 5

Sounds (all)
when functioning as nonsyllabics

Nonsyllabic vocoids   Nonsyllabic contoids
(consonants)

Trills are most conveniently classified as special types of partial stricture rather than as closures. Taken as a unit, a trill gives an impression of continuity; it allows an escape of air; its automatic repetition differentiates it from specific repetitions of the closures of stops, so that the trill must be analyzed as a unified whole, not a sequence of unrelated closures. Now with lung air, no oral stop can exist while the velic is open, else air will escape in a continuous stream from the nose; by definition that prevents trills from being classified with stops, since they have an air stream that is completely capped. The sound made by opening the velic during stop production is a nasal (e.g. [b] is changed to [m] in the sequence [bm]). With trills this is not true; an alveolar trill, for example, remains that same trill and retains all its essential characteristics if the velic is open — it simply becomes qualified by the addition of nasal timbre, as would any other oral continuant, such as [i] or [l] or [z].

In vibratory trills the impression of continuity and unity (with no acoustic separation of the percussions) is enhanced. With these there can be no doubt of their essential classification with the continuants. To list voice with any deliberate (and essentially slow) non-automatic repeated closing and opening of the vocal cords in a series of lung-air glottal stops would be unthinkable.

Like other continuants, trills can be of fricative or frictionless varieties. The latter type is clear, and " liquid," whereas the former is very " breathy." In the one the release between closures leaves a cavity stricture, so that no friction is audible, whereas in the other the release is to a position which gives local friction. Both types appear in language; an alveolar frictionless trill is used in Spanish; approximately the same position is employed in Mixteco for a phoneme which has a fricative trill as one variant.

When certain articulatory positions of the vocal organs are taken, a shrill penetrating sound results, called a *whistle*. No articulatory criterion can be given by the author to state at exactly what point the shifting position of the tongue or lips (or even the pharynx and glottis) may change continuants into whistles. In this respect the *whistle point*, like the friction point, must be established by an acoustic criterion rather than an articulatory one. When a formation whistles, it whistles — as anyone knows who after long arduous practice finally passes the whistle point in some continuant, only to be perplexed to determine what change was finally made just as the whistle came.

The average whistle is a kind of double vocoid in which the front labial partial stricture is of a special type that gives *whistle timbre* while the lingual stricture controls the pitch. Lingual strictures of at least two general types are found, depending on the individual. In one type (my own) high pitch is attained by high front tongue positions similar to that for [i], while low pitches have tongue positions analogous to that for [u]. In another type the tongue is highly grooved; low pitch is obtained by a backing of the tongue, high pitch by its fronting (somewhat analogous to [s] versus [ʃ]). Pitch may be controlled in at least a third manner: very sharp retroflexion may provide the low tones, whereas the lowering of the tip to more normal position raises the pitch.

Dental whistles use both labial and lingual vocoidal modifications for pitch; rounding of the lips gives lower pitches than unrounding. The only pharyngeal whistle which the author has heard was made by Dr. Fritz Frauchiger; it was produced while the mouth was wide open and appeared to come from the throat. It seems possible that " whistle voice " uses a whistle formation of the vocal cords rather than a type of glottal vibratory trill. The author has never heard this type of singing. Whistles may be made by pharynx air and mouth air as well as by lung air; in this respect they differ from other vocoids, which tend to be of zero type with any mechanism except the pulmonic one or except directly after the release of mouth-air or pharynx-air stops.

Whistles may have two distinct tones audible at once. The *double whistle point* can at present be only acoustically established. The articulatory formations seem to differ but little from those giving single whistles.

Whistles may combine with many other types of articulation. One of the most beautiful, used for imitation of bird calls, combines a labial whistle with a (voiceless) uvular trill. Of course whistles can be modified by nasalization, voice, and the like. They can be frictionalized in various ways, or in turn modify oral local friction.

The strictures that control the egress of an air stream may have various degrees of closure which can be described in relation to assumed norms, or norms of an articulatory or acoustic nature. Combinations of strictures in the different cavities allow different degrees of air escape as they interrupt the air stream in various ways which provide characteristic acoustic effects. Classification and designation of sound types allow for these characteristic differences in degree of strictural closure of a passageway or a combination of passageways.

CHAPTER VIII

CONCLUSIONS

IN THE preceding chapters of this study various articulatory movements have been described which cause vocal sounds and modify them. The later part of the chapter in hand, instead of discussing parts of sounds or attempting to abstract and analyze individually their productive movements, will indicate a procedure for describing sounds as complete wholes by giving a statement of certain features which should be included in each description. Up to this point all vocal sounds have been treated without reference to the fact that they may or may not be used in linguistic systems. Assuming that a sufficiently large sampling has been taken of speech sounds to insure the inclusion of most of the major types which can be found, a tentative statement can now be given of the line of demarcation between speech and nonspeech types.

SPEECH SOUNDS VERSUS NONSPEECH SOUNDS

A greater difference is seen between speech sounds and nonspeech sounds within their usage of productive mechanisms than within their controlling mechanisms. Induction and scraping production mechanisms apparently are never used significantly in speech. Percussion mechanisms occur in speech only when they function simultaneously with air-stream mechanisms either by superimposing their sounds upon these mechanisms during the opening and closing of stops or by causing oral static percussives during a velar stop which has pulmonic or pharyngeal pressure — that is, the first release of double stops.

Within the air-stream mechanisms there are further differences between nonspeech and speech sound types. Minor air mechanisms are never used in a system of speech sounds except where belch timbre and esophageal air are substituted for voice and lung air in the speech of laryngectomized patients. The major air mechanisms are all used in speech; ingressive lung air appears to be employed only for variants of phonemes in surprise, pain, or occasionally in certain types of

149

rapid speech, and the like;[1] ingressive pharynx air is almost limited to combinations with lung air; egressive mouth air perhaps does not occur except in exclamations.

It seems that only two combinations of major air mechanisms occur in speech, the pulmonic mechanism with the pharyngeal one and the pulmonic mechanism with the oral mechanism. In these combinations the lung air seems always to be egressive and voiced.

A further limitation appears to exist in regard to the number of phonemes which can be produced in uninterrupted sequence by a single-direction initiator movement of any one major air mechanism. With all of these air mechanisms the number is limited by the length of time which the initiator can keep moving in order to expel air. Since the lungs as initiator can continue contracting much longer than the larynx can continue rising or the tongue fronting, more sounds can be produced in a sequence with that mechanism. It appears, however, that no more than one phoneme is made by any single-direction movement of the pharyngeal and oral initiators. Nasalized, aspirated, and voiced clicks may comprise more than single phonemes, but in these cases the extra phonemes of nasalized, aspirated, and voiced releases are supplied by the pulmonic system.

The controlling mechanisms of nonspeech sounds are quite similar to those of speech sounds. The difference is largely due to the fact that extreme departures from a normal position of articulation or exaggerated types of movement occur sometimes in nonspeech sounds but rarely if ever within phonemic norms.

Processes of segmentation are the same for speech and nonspeech sounds. Both groups use the same articulators. Furthermore, the shapes of the articulators are usually of the same types except that odd shapes such as that of the tongue twisted lengthwise are not known in speech. Points of articulation are similar for the two groups except that extreme displacements do not occur in speech (e.g. the tongue tip against the uvula). Types of articulation movements are likewise the same except that spasmodic forms (e.g. for belches, sneezes, hiccoughs, and some kinds of langhter), involuntary chat-

---

[1] I have heard Dr. Charles Voegelin mention an ingressive vowel, however, which is said to occur in Maidu; if it is there the normal form of the phoneme, then ingressive lung air is used as a phonemic norm, and this restriction could be omitted.

ters, and other sorts of involuntary movement do not produce speech norms; this group of spasmodically formed sounds includes a considerable percentage of those which are resultant from momentary physiological states. Strictural function can be analyzed according to just one set of principles for all types of speech and nonspeech sounds. Degrees of stricture fall into the same general classes for both groups, and strictures interrupt the air stream in similar ways regardless of whether or not the sounds are used in speech.

A DESCRIPTIVE ORDER

For the systematic description of any sound, the following items should be mentioned when their action is above the threshold of perception: A statement should appear describing the type of mechanism by which the sound is made — whether by an air-stream mechanism, percussion mechanism, induction mechanism, or scraping mechanism. If an air mechanism is basic to the sound, note should be made of the position of the initiator and the direction of its movement, the presence of any valvate strictures, and the degree to which the air stream is interrupted. When above the perceptual threshold, acme, primary, subprimary, secondary, tertiary, and adjunct strictures must be described with a rough statement of their points of articulation, types of articulation, shapes of the articulators, and degrees of closure. If two mechanisms combine to make the sound, the features of each mechanism must be described separately. The syllable function sound should be stated.

One illustration will be given of this type of description: A palatalized [b] is made with an air-stream mechanism. The lungs are the initiator and have egressive movement. A secondary valvate closure is at the velic and a subvalvate closure is at the esophageal orifice. The air stream is completely capped, so the sound is a stop. The acme stricture is the primary one. The primary stricture has labial point of articulation, a normal type of articulating movement, and flat shape, with complete closure. The subprimary stricture has palatal articulation, a normal type of articulating movement, and humped shape, with a modifying cavity-friction degree of closure. The tertiary stricture has glottal point of articulation, vibratory trill type of articulating movement, flat shape, with a qualifying partial degree of cavity-friction closure. The subprimary stricture has a subprimary adjunct that has a normal type of complete contact at the sides of the tongue.

Some of the characteristics of the [b] which have been left undescribed in the preceding paragraph, and which therefore are subsumed under this articulatory label as a layer of imitation-label material which can only be known by an observer after hearing the sound, are the exact point of the palate below which the hump of the tongue occurs; the exact height of the tongue; the exact shape of the tongue; the position of the tip of the tongue; the position of the root of the tongue; the position of the faucal pillars; the position of the epiglottis; the position of the false vocal cords; the position of the back pharyngeal wall; the relative strength of the articulating movements; the relative loudness of the sound; the relative duration of the strictures; the presence of a passive nasal chamber; the presence of a passive esophageal chamber. The sound was made in isolation, not as part of a sequence of sounds, and with no release of the oral or velic strictures. Therefore there could be no mention of its semipassive chambers or releasing strictures; or of gliding movements connecting it to other sounds; or of anticipatory movements for it or for other sounds; or of the type of segment, segment crest, segment trough, crossing glide, bulge of stricture, time bulge, or percussion transition; or of its relation to a syllable, syllabic, nonsyllabic, arresting segment, or trigger segment (except that the sound is a syllabic and comprises a syllable itself); or of its relation to a stress group; and so on.

The fact may be emphasized that no phonetic description, no matter how detailed, is complete. The description of sounds in the manner suggested here includes the major elements which are above the perceptual threshold of a particular observer and delineates the basic productive and controlling factors of mechanisms, air streams, and strictures. The descriptive technic identifies neither the exact acoustic nature nor the exact articulatory nature of the sounds, but it does serve to give a rough analysis of their basic productive and controlling features.

To facilitate convenience in reference and to approximate traditional nomenclature more closely, the description is modified in two ways: (1) Every explicit statement is omitted if the item which it mentions can be subsumed under some other part of the label. " Voiced," for example, implies glottal point of articulation, with a type of articulation which constitutes a vibratory trill, and frictionless degree of partial closure. " Nasalized," when describing clicks, implies the presence of a second air mechanism which has lung initiator, egressive air stream, vibrating vocal cords, and open nasal passage. (2) The descriptive order is reversed. Qualifiers are mentioned first, beginning with the ones of lowest rank and working progressively toward the acme stricture; the acme stricture follows the qualifiers; secondary or primary valvate strictures come next, if mentioned at all (all sounds are assumed to have a secondary valvate stricture unless some term such as " nasal " prevents this assumption); direction of the air stream is then noted (and is taken to be egressive unless some factor specifically states or implies otherwise; " click," for example, implies ingressive air stream); choice of initiator, or major air mechanism, is next in order (voiceless egressive lung air is assumed unless some factor implies otherwise); the final item states the degree of interruption of the air stream and the subclassification of the type if the sound is a continuant (if under the primary stricture it does not prove convenient to mention the degree of closure, this final item will usually imply it for partial strictures).

A few names may be given to illustrate the results of utilizing this convenient abbreviated type of labeling for the description of vocal sounds:

> Voiced palatalized bilabial stop
> Voiced alveolar lateral fricative
> Voiced bilabial nasal
> Voiced high front vocoid
> Velar stop
> Alveolar grooved fricative (or alveolar sibilant)
> Nasalized alveolar click stop

One can apply a symbol to each or to many of the factors listed for description. This produces a type of analphabetic notation in terms of productive and controlling mechanisms. It adds little to the data included in the more common type of abbreviated description just given but has some value for calling to one's attention the many assumptions implicit in short labels. Of course, even an analphabetic system is limited to noting those elements which are above the perceptual threshold of the observer; it is suggestive, but by no means exhaustive.

FUNCTIONAL ANALPHABETIC SYMBOLISM

M productive mechanism
  p percussion mechanism
  i induction mechansim
  s scraping mechanism
  a air-stream mechanism
    I initiator
      l for lung air
      p for pharynx air
      m for mouth air
      mm for a minor mech-
        anism
        e for esophageal air
    D direction of the air stream
      e egressive
      i ingressive
C controlling mechanism
  V valvate stricture
    v velic stricture
    o oral stricture
    e subvalvate esophageal
      stricture
    g subvalvate glottal stricture
  I degree of air-stream interrup-
    tion
    c complete (stops)
    p partial (continuants)
      f frictional
      v nonfrictional
      o fricative oral
        c central
        l lateral
      r resonant oral
        c central (vocoid)
        l lateral
      n nasal
        n resonant nasal
        f fricative nasal
  Rank of stricture
  A acme
  P primary
  Ps subprimary
  S secondary
  T tertiary
  j adjunct
  Features of stricture
  p point of articulation
    l labial
    d dental
    i interdental

  a alveolar
  p palatal
  s velar
  u uvular
  v velic
  f faucal
  h pharyngeal
  g glottal
  w arytenoid
  e esophageal
a articulator
  l lips
  d teeth
  t tongue tip
  c blade of tongue
  m middle or front part of
    tongue
  a mid-back part of
    tongue
  b back part of tongue
  r root of tongue
  s velum
  u uvula
  v velic
  f faucal pillars
  h pharyngeal wall
  i epiglottis
  g vocal cords
  w arytenoid cartilages
  e orifice of the esophagus
d degrees of articulation
  t in time
    l long
    n normal
    s short
  e extensive (region: front
    to back)
  r restricted
  n narrow (side to side)
  w wide
  h high
    c close
    o open
  m mid
    c close
    o open
  l low
    c close
    o open

f with local friction
v with cavity friction
w with whistle timbre
t types of articulation
  n normal
  f flap
  i iterative
    c chatter
    t trill
      v vibratory trill
      z laryngealization
      p pitch
        h high
        m medium or
          normal
        l low
  f false types
  s spasmodic
r relative strengths
  a of articulating move-
    ments
    f fortis
    n normal
    l lenis
  s of acoustic impressions
    l loud
    n normal
    s soft
s shapes of articulators
  f flat
  g grooved
  r rounded
  c convex
  o contracted
  e expanded
  s straight

  u cupped
  r retroflexed
  h humped
  a retracted
  p protruded
  n with central air escape
  l with lateral air escape
j adjuncts
  c central
  l unilateral
  ll bilateral
    e extensive contact
    s slight contact
S segmental type
  c crest
  t trough
  g crossing glide
  b bulge of stricture
  t time bulge
  i instrumental
  r real
  p perceptual
F function phonetically
  S of the segment in the syllable
    v vowel
    s syllabic contoid
    n nonsyllabic vocoid
    c consonant
    t trigger segment
    a arresting segment
    p presyllabic
    o postsyllabic
  G of a syllable in a stress group
    h heavily stressed
    m moderately stressed
    w weakly stressed

A few formulas may be given to illustrate the application of this analphabetic system. The stops are unreleased segments. Since the sounds are all in isolation each one constitutes a syllable.

[t]: *M*aIIDe*C*VveIc*AP p*aatd*tlt*n*r*an*sf*s*SiFS*s

[f]: *M*aIIDe*C*VveIpfoc*AP p*da*l*d*tlft*n*r*an*s*n*sf S*r*p*F*Ss

[n]: *M*aIIDe*C*Voe*I*pvnn*AP p*aatd*tlt*n*r*an*s*n*sf*S *p*va*v*d*tlvt*n*r*an*sss*f*T *p*gag*d*tlwv*t*i*t*v*r*a-
n*s*n*sf*S*r*p*F*Ss

[o]: *M*aIIDe*C*VveIpv*r*c*AP p*la*l*d*tl*wmov*t*n*r*an*s*n*s*r*j*lls*AP p*sab*d*tlmc*t*n*r*an*s*n*sf*T *p*gag-
d*tl*wv*t*i*t*v*r*an*s*n*s*f*S*r*p*F*S*v

Labialized [s]: *M*aIlDe*C*veIpfoc*AP*p*aacd*tleftn*r*ansnsgjlleP*sp*laldtlwmovtn*r*ans-n*s*rjllsSrp*F*Ss

Bilabial click stop: *M*aImDi*C*Ic*AP*p*laldtltn*r*ansf*Si*FSs

Voiced bilabial implosive stop: *M*aIpDi*C*veIc*AP*p*laldtntn*r*ansnsf/*M*aIlDe*C*Vv-eIc*AP*p*laldtntn*r*ansnsfT*p*gagdtnwvtitv*r*ansnsfSrp*F*Ss

These formulas conclude the monograph. To trace through their symbols is to see the unfolding of a phonetic theory which attempts to set forth the interrelated phenomena that contribute to the production of vocal sounds. The most significant usage of these sounds is as speech signals. Yet the intricacies of speech systems are best understood by viewing them in the light of a phonetic but nonlinguistic analysis of the most basic of all speech subunits — the segments. Segments may be combined into larger units, that is, into phonemes, which are the basic speech units that make up the morphemes, words, and phrases of grammar. The analysis of phonemes requires a separate type of treatment from that presented here. The analytical procedures of phonemics have already provided us with the requisite technics. Even these practices, however, may well be modified and clarified by correlating them with a more rigorous phonetic theory than has so far been available. The present study prepares the way, therefore, for a reformulation of phonemic statement.

BIBLIOGRAPHY

ACOUST. SOC. AM., " Report of Committee on Acoustical Standardization," *Journ. Acoust. Soc. Am.,* 2 (1931), 311–24. See also "American Standard Acoustical Terminology," *ibid.,* 14 (1942), 84–101.

AIKIN, W. A., *The Voice, an Introduction to Practical Phonology.* London, 1927.

ANDERSON, V. A., " The Auditory Memory Span for Speech Sounds," *Speech Monographs,* 5 (1938), 115–29.

ANDRADE, M. J., " Some Questions of Fact and Policy concerning Phonemes," *Lang.,* 12 (1936), 1–14.

ARMSTRONG, L. E., *The Phonetics of French.* London, 1932.

BÁRÁNY, E., " Transposition of Speech Sounds," *Journ. Acoust. Soc. Am.,* 8 (1937), 217–19.

BARKER, M. L., *A Handbook of German Intonation for University Students.* New York, 1926.

BARTHOLOMEW, W. T., *Acoustics of Music.* New York, 1942.

—— " Physical Definition of Good Voice Quality in the Male Voice," *Journ. Acoust. Soc. Am.,* 6 (1931), 25–33.

BEACH, D. M., *The Phonetics of the Hottentot Language.* Cambridge, 1938.

BELL, A. M., *Sounds and Their Relations.* New York, 1887.

—— *Visible Speech, the Science of Universal Alphabetics,* Inaugural Edition. London, 1867.

BENDER, J. F., AND KLEINFELD, V. M., *Speech Correction Manual, Containing 317 Practical Drills for Speech and Voice Improvement.* New York, 1936.

BERGEN, E., *How to Become a Ventriloquist.* New York, 1938.

BLACK, J. W., " Effect of the Consonant on the Vowel," *Journ. Acoust. Soc. Am.,* 19 (1939), 203–5.

—— " The Stability of the Vowel," *Speech Monographs,* 25 (1939), 52–57.

—— " Vowel Quality before and after an Operation for an Occluded Nasal Passage," *ibid.,* 5 (1938), 62–64.

BLOCH, B., Review of " Phonetic Transcriptions from 'American Speech,' " Edited by J. D. Zimmerman, *Lang.,* 16 (1940), 172–75.

—— AND TRAGER, GEORGE L., *Outline of Linguistic Analysis.* Special Publications of the Linguistic Society of America. Baltimore, 1942.

—— —— *Tables for a System of Phonetic Description,* Preliminary Edition. New Haven, 1940.

BLOOMER, H., AND SHOHARA, H. H., "The Study of Respiratory Movements by Roentgen Kymography," *Speech Monographs*, 8 (1941), 91–101.

BLOOMFIELD, L., *Language*. New York, 1933.

—— "Menomini Morphophonemics," *Études phonologiques dédiées à la mémoire de M. le prince N. S. Trubetzkoy. Travaux du Cercle linguistique de Prague*, Vol. 8. Prague, 1939.

—— *Outline Guide for the Practical Study of Foreign Languages*. Special Publications of the Linguistic Society of America. Baltimore, 1942.

BLUEMEL, C. S., *Stammering and Cognate Defects of Speech*, 2 vols. New York, 1913.

BOAS, F., *Handbook of American Indian Languages*. Smithsonian Institution, Bureau of American Ethnology, Bulletin 40. Washington, 1911.

BRØNDAL, V., "Sound and Phoneme," *Proceedings of the Second International Congress of Phonetic Sciences*. Cambridge, 1936.

CARHART, R. T., "Air-Flow through the Larynx," *Quart. Journ. Speech*, 26 (1940), 606–14.

—— "Infra-glottal Resonance and a Cushion-pipe," *Speech Monographs*, 5 (1938), 65–96.

—— "The Spectra of Model Larynx Tones," *ibid.*, 8 (1941), 76–84.

CARMODY, F. J., "Radiographs of Thirteen German Vowels," *Arch. Néer. Phon. Expér.*, 12 (1936), 27–33.

—— "An X-Ray Study of Pharyngeal Articulation," *Univ. Calif. Publ. Mod. Philol.*, 21, No. 5 (1941), 377–84.

CATFORD, J. C., "On the Classification of Stop Consonants," *Le Maître Phonétique*, 3d Series, 65 (1939), 2–5.

COTTON, J. C., "Syllabic Rate, a New Concept in the Study of Speech Rate Variation," *Speech Monographs*, 3 (1936), 112–17.

—— "Tongue Movements and Vowel Quality," *ibid.*, 4 (1937), 38–43.

COWAN, M., *Pitch and Intensity Characteristics of Stage Speech, Arch. Speech*, 1, Supplement (1936).

—— Review of "Experiments of Trendelenburg, Wullstein, and Hartman," *Journ. Acoust. Soc. Am.*, 11 (1940), 380–81. Abstract only.

CUNNINGHAM, D. J., *Text-book of Anatomy*, Seventeenth Edition. New York, 1937.

CURRY, R., *The Mechanism of the Human Voice*. New York, 1940.

—— "The Physiology of the Contralto Voice," *Arch. Néer. Phon. Expér.*, 14 (1938), 73–79.

—— "Speech Recording and Analysis with the Cathode Ray Oscillograph," *ibid.*, 11 (1935), 107–18.

CURRY, S. S., *Mind and Voice, Principles and Methods in Vocal Training*. Boston, 1910.

DAVIS, E. B., " Nasal Twang," *Le Maître Phonétique*, 3d Series, 56 (1941), 4–5.

DE GROOT, A. W., " Instrumental Phonetics. Its Value for Linguists," *K. Akademie van Wetenschappen, Afdeelingen Letterkunde, Mededeelingen*, 65, A. 2 (1928), 37–96. Amsterdam.

DENSMORE, F., *The American Indians and Their Music*. New York, 1926.

DE SAUSSURE, F., *Cours de linguistique générale*, Third Edition. Paris, 1931.

DE V. PIENAAR, P., " Click Formation and Distribution," *Proceedings of the Third International Congress of Phonetic Sciences* (1939), 345–51.

DOKE, C. M., " Notes on a Problem in the Mechanism of the Zulu Clicks," *Bantu Studies*, 2 (1923), 43–45.

—— " An Outline of the Phonetics of the Language of the Ch̃ũ: Bushmen of North-West Kalahari," *ibid.*, 2, No. 3 (1925), 129–65.

—— *The Phonetics of the Zulu Language, ibid.*, Vol. 2, Special Number. Johannesburg, 1926.

DREW, R. O., AND KELLOGG, E. W., " Starting Characteristics of Speech Sounds," *Journ. Acoust. Soc. Am.*, 12 (1940), 95–103.

DUYFF, J., " Petite contribution à la connaissance de la voix de fausset," *Arch. Néer. Phon. Expér.*, 4 (1929), 67–71.

EIJKMAN, L. P. H., " The Interior Larynx in Song and Speech," *Archiv für vergleichende Phonetik*, 1 (1937), 78–89.

—— AND WIERSMA, C. A. G., " The Influence of the Subglottal Passage and the Nasal Cavity on Non-nasal Speech-sounds," *Arch. Néer. Phon. Expér.*, 11 (1935), 29–38.

ELLIS, A. J., *The Essentials of Phonetics* [with annotated bibliography]. London, 1848.

—— " On Early English Pronunciation," *Early English Text Society*, Extra Series, Nos. 2, 7, 14, 23, 56. London, 1869–89.

—— *Pronunciation for Singers, with Especial Reference to the English, German, Italian, and French Languages*. London, 1877.

EMENEAU, M. B., " The Vowels of the Badaga Language," *Lang.*, 15 (1939), 43–47.

Études phonologiques dédiées à la mémoire de M. le prince N. S. Trubetzkoy. Travaux du Cercle linguistique de Prague, Vol. 8. Prague, 1939.

FAIRBANKS, G., AND PRONOVOST, W., " An Experimental Study of the Pitch Characteristics of the Voice during the Expression of the Emotions," *Speech Monographs*, 6 (1939), 87–104.

FLETCHER, H., " Loudness, Masking and Their Relations to the Hearing Process and the Problem of Noise Measurement," *Journ. Acoust. Soc. Am.*, 9 (1938), 275–93.

—— *Speech and Hearing*. London, 1929.

FORCHHAMMER, H., *How to Learn Danish*, Fourth Edition. Copenhagen, 1932.

FORCHHAMMER, J., *Die Grundlage der Phonetik*. Heidelberg, 1924.

FRY, A. H., Review of "Phonetics and Phonology," by B. Faddegon, *Lang.*, 16 (1940), 164–67.

GAIRDNER, W. H. T., *The Phonetics of Arabic*. London, 1925.

GANTHONY, R., *Practical Ventriloquism and Its Sister Arts*, Third Edition, Revised by Will Goldston. London [1920].

GEMELLI, A., AND PASTORI, G., "Analyse électrique du langage," *Arch. Néer. Phon. Expér.*, 10 (1934), 1–29.

GRAFF, W. L., "Remarks on the Phoneme," *Am. Speech*, 10 (1935), 83–87.

GRAMMONT, M., *Traité de phonétique*. Paris, 1933.

GRANDGENT, C. H., *German and English Sounds*. Boston, 1892.

—— *Old and New*. Cambridge, 1920.

GRAY, H., *Anatomy of the Human Body*, Twenty-third Edition. Philadelphia, 1936.

GUTHRIE, D., "Physiology of the Vocal Mechanism," *Brit. Med. Journ.*, No. 4066 (1938), 1189–95.

HAAS, M. R., "Ablaut and Its Function in Muskogee," *Lang.*, 16 (1940), 141–50.

HADEN, E. F., *The Physiology of French Consonant Changes*. Supplement to *Language*, Dissertation 26. Baltimore, 1938.

HALL, H. H., "Sound Analysis," *Journ. Acoust. Soc. Am.*, 8 (1937), 257–62.

HARRIS, Z. S., Review of "Foundations of Language," by L. H. Gray, *Lang.*, 16 (1940), 216–31.

HEEPE, M., *Lautzeichen und ihre Anwendung in verschiedenen Sprachgebieten*. Berlin, 1928.

HERRIOTT, W., "High Speed Motion Picture Photography," *Bell System Tech. Journ.*, 17 (1938), 393–405.

HERZOG, G., "Speech Melody and Primitive Music," *Musical Quarterly*, 20 (1934), 452–66.

HOWELL, W. H., *A Textbook of Physiology*, Fourteenth Edition. Philadelphia, 1940.

HUDGINS, C. V., AND STETSON, R. H., "Voicing of Consonants by Depression of the Larynx," *Arch. Néer. Phon. Expér.*, 11 (1935), 1–28.

HUIZINGA, E., "Recherches sur un ventriloque néerlandais," *Arch. Néer. Phon. Expér.*, 6 (1931), 66–87.

JACKSON, C. L., "The Voice after Direct Laryngoscopic Operations, Laryngofissure and Laryngectomy," *Arch. of Otolaryngol.*, 31 (1940), 23–36.

JESPERSEN, O., *The Articulations of Speech Sounds Represented by Means of Analphabetic Symbols*. Marburg in Hessen, 1889.

—— *Language, Its Nature, Development and Origin*. London, 1922.

—— *Lehrbuch der Phonetik*, Fourth Edition. Leipzig, 1926.

JESPERSEN, O., *Phonetische Grundfragen.* Leipzig, 1904.

JOHNSON, T. E., *Introductory Phonetics.* University, Alabama, 1942.

JONES, D., *An English Pronouncing Dictionary,* Revised Edition. London and Toronto, 1924.

—— " Implosive and Click Sounds," *Le Maître Phonétique,* 22 (1907), 111–14.

—— *An Outline of English Phonetics,* Fourth Edition. New York, 1934.

—— AND WOO, K. T., *A Cantonese Phonetic Reader.* London, 1912.

JONES, S., " The Perceptibility of Sounds," *Le Maître Phonétique,* 3d Series, 41 (1926), 4–6.

JOZEN, P., *Des principes de l'écriture phonétique et des moyens d'arriver à une orthographie rationnelle et une écriture universelle.* Paris, 1877.

KANTNER, C. E., AND WEST, R., *Phonetics.* New York, 1941.

KARLGREN, B., *A Mandarin Phonetic Reader, in the Pekinese Dialect, with an Introductory Essay on the Pronunciation. Archives d'Études Orientales,* Vol. 13. Upsala, 1917.

KARR, HARRISON M., *Your Speaking Voice.* Glendale, 1938.

KENYON, J. S., *American Pronunciation, a Textbook of Phonetics for Students of English,* Sixth Edition. Ann Arbor, 1935.

KIMBER, D. C., GRAY, C. E., AND STACKPOLE, C. E., *Textbook of Anatomy and Physiology,* Tenth Edition. New York, 1938.

KINZIE, C. E., AND KINZIE, R., *Lip-Reading for the Deafened Adult.* Philadelphia, 1931.

KLINGHARDT, H., *Artikulations- und Hörübungen.* Cöthen, 1914.

—— AND DE FOURMESTRAUX, M., *French Intonation Exercises,* Translated and Adapted for English Readers by M. L. Barker. New York, 1923.

KOCK, W. E., " Certain Subjective Phenomena Accompanying a Frequency Vibrato," *Journ. Acoust. Soc. Am.,* 8 (1936), 23–25.

KRAPP, G. P., *The Pronunciation of Standard English in America.* New York, 1919.

KURATH, H., with the collaboration of M. L. Hansen, J. Bloch, B. Bloch, *Handbook of the Linguistic Geography of New England.* Providence, 1939.

—— with the collaboration of M. L. Hanley, B. Bloch, M. L. Hansen, G. A. Lowman, Jr., *Linguistic Atlas of New England,* Vol. I. Providence, 1939.

LARSEN, T., AND WALKER, F. C., *Pronunciation, a Practical Guide to American Standards.* London, 1930.

LEVIN, N. M., " Speech following Total Laryngectomy (without the Aid of the Mechanical Larynx)," a paper read before the Northern Medical Society. Philadelphia, 1939.

LEWIS, D., " Vocal Resonance," *Journ. Acoust. Soc. Am.,* 8 (1936), 91–99.

LEWIS, D., COWAN, M., AND FAIRBANKS, G., " Pitch and Frequency Modulation," *Journ. Exper. Psychol.*, 27 (1940), 23–36.

LOUNSBURY, T. R., *The Standard of Pronunciation in English*. New York, 1904.

LOWIE, R. H., " Hidatsa Texts, Collected by Robert H. Lowie; with Grammatical Notes and Phonograph Transcriptions by Zellig Harris and C. F. Voegelin," *Prehistory Research Series*, Vol. 1, No. 6. Indianapolis, 1939.

LUTHY, C. T., *The Human Speech Sounds*. Peoria, 1918.

McLEAN, M. P., *Good American Speech*, Revised Edition. New York, 1930.

MENZERATH, P., AND DE LACERDA, A., *Koartikulation, Steuerung und Lautabgrenzung; eine experimentelle Untersuchung*. Berlin, 1933.

MILLER, C. B., *An Experimental-phonetic Investigation of Whispered Conversation, Considered from the Linguistic Point of View*. Bochum-Langendreer, 1934.

MILLER, D. C., *The Science of Musical Sounds*. New York, 1916.

MILLET, A., *Précis d'expérimentation phonétique*. Paris, 1926.

MONTGOMERY, H. C., " An Optical Harmonic Analyzer," *Bell System Tech. Journ.*, 17 (1938), 406–15.

MORRISON, W. W., AND FINEMAN, S., " Production of Pseudo-voice after Total Laryngectomy," *Trans. Am. Acad. Opthalmol. and Otolaryngol.*, 41 (1936), 631–34.

MOSES, E. R., JR., "A Brief History of Palatography," *Quart. Journ. Speech*, 26 (1940), 615–25.

MUCKEY, F. S., *The Natural Method of Voice Production*. New York, 1915.

MURPHY, O. J., " Time Intervals in Telephone Conversation," *Bell Lab. Rec.*, 17 (1939), 85.

NAVARRO TOMÁS, T., *Manual de pronunciación española*, Fourth Edition. Publicaciones de la Revista de Filología Española. Madrid, 1918.

—— AND ESPINOSA, A. M., *A Primer of Spanish Pronunciation*. New York, 1926.

NEGUS, V. E., *The Mechanism of the Larynx*. St. Louis, 1929.

NICHOLSON, G. G., *A Practical Introduction to French Phonetics, for the Use of English-speaking Students and Teachers*. London, 1909.

NOËL-ARMFIELD, G., *General Phonetics, for Missionaries and Students of Languages*, Fourth Edition. Cambridge, 1931.

PANCONCELLI-CALZIA, G., *Einführung in die angewandte Phonetik*. Berlin, 1914.

PARMENTER, C. E., AND TREVIÑO, S. N., " Vowel Positions as Shown by X-Rays," *Quart. Journ. Speech*, 18 (1932), 351–69.

—— —— " The Length of the Sounds of a Middle Westerner," *Am. Speech*, 10 (1935), 129–33.

PASSY, P., *Petite phonétique comparée des principales langues européennes*, Third Edition. Leipzig, 1922.

PASSY, P., *The Sounds of the French Language, Their Formation, Combination and Representation*, Second Edition, Translated by D. L. Savory and D. Jones. Oxford, 1914.

"Pedro the Voder, a Machine That Talks," *Bell Lab. Rec.*, 17 (1939), 170–71.

PEPINSKY, A., "The Laryngeal Ventricle Considered as an Acoustical Filter," *Journ. Acoust. Soc. Am.*, 14 (1942), 32–35.

Phonetic Transcription of Indian Languages, The. Smithsonian Miscellaneous Collections, Vol. 66, No. 6. Washington, 1916.

PIKE, K. L., *Phonemic Work Sheet*. Siloam Springs, 1938.

Practical Orthography of African Languages, Memorandum I, Revised Edition. International Institute of African Languages and Cultures. London, 1930.

Principles of the International Phonetic Association, The (including a chart revised to 1932), Supplement to *Le Maître Phonétique*. London, 1912.

Proceedings of the Second International Congress of Phonetic Sciences, Edited by D. Jones and D. B. Fry. Cambridge, 1936.

Proceedings of the Third International Congress of Phonetic Sciences, Edited by E. Blancquaert and W. Pée. Ghent, 1939.

RIPMAN, W., *Elements of Phonetics, English, French and German*, Translated and Adapted by W. Ripman from Prof. Viëtor's *Kleine Phonetik*. London, 1899.

ROOT, A. R., "Pitch-Patterns and Tonal Movement in Speech," *Psychological Monographs*, 40, No. 1 (1930), 109–59.

ROSITZKE, H. A., "Vowel-Length in General American Speech," *Lang.*, 15 (1939), 99–109.

ROUSSELOT, P. J., *Principes de phonétique expérimentale*, New Edition. Paris, 1924.

RUSSELL, G. O., "The Mechanism of Speech," *Journ. Acoust. Soc. Am.*, 1 (1929), 83–109.

—— *Speech and Voice, with X-Rays of English, French, German, Italian, Spanish, Soprano, Tenor, and Baritone Subjects*. New York, 1931.

—— *The Vowel. Its Physiological Mechanism as Shown by X-Ray*. Columbus, 1928.

SAPIR, E., "Glottalized Continuants in Navaho, Nootka, and Kwakiutl (with a Note on Indo-European)," *Lang.*, 14 (1938), 248–74.

—— *Language, an Introduction to the Study of Speech*. New York, 1921.

—— "Notes on the Gweabo Language of Liberia," *Lang.*, 7 (1931), 30–41.

—— "Sound Patterns in Language," *Lang.*, 1 (1925), 37–51.

SCHALL, L. A., "Psychology of Laryngectomized Patients," *Arch. of Otolaryngol.*, 28 (1938), 581–84.

SCRIPTURE, E. W., *The Elements of Experimental Phonetics*. New York, 1902.

SCRIPTURE, E. W., *Researches in Experimental Phonetics, the Study of Speech Curves*. Washington, 1906.

SEASHORE, C. E., *Psychology of Music*. New York and London, 1938.

SHOHARA, H. H., " An Experimental Study of the Control of Pronunciation," *Speech Monographs*, 6 (1939), 105–9.

SIEVERS, E., *Grundzüge der Phonetik*, Fourth Edition. In *Bibliothek indogermanischer Grammatiken*, Vol. I. Leipzig, 1893.

SNOW, W. B., " Change of Pitch with Loudness at Low Frequencies," *Journ. Acoust. Soc. Am.*, 8 (1936), 14–19.

SOAMES, L., *Introduction to English, French and German Phonetics*, Third Edition, Revised and Partly Rewritten by W. Viëtor. London, 1913.

" Some Orthographic Recommendations, Arising Out of Discussions by a Group of Six Americanist Linguists," *Am. Anthropol.*, 36 (1934), 629–63.

STETSON, R. H., " The Breathing Movements in Singing," *Arch. Néer. Phon. Expér.*, 6 (1931), 115–64.

—— " Epsophageal Speech for Any Laryngectomized Patient," *Arch. of Otolaryngol.*, 26 (1937), 132–42.

—— *Motor Phonetics, a Study of Speech Movements in Action*, *Arch. Néer. Phon. Expér*, Vol. 3. La Haye, 1928.

—— " Oesophageal Speech. Methods of Instruction after Laryngectomy," *ibid.*, 13 (1937), 95–110.

—— " Speech Movements in Action," *Trans. Am. Laryngol. Assn.*, 55 (1933), 29–42.

—— AND FULLER, F. L., " Diphthong Formation," *Arch. Néer. Phon. Expér.*, 5 (1930), 31–36.

—— AND HUDGINS, C. V., " Functions of the Breathing Movements in the Mechanism of Speech," *ibid.*, 5 (1930), 1–30.

—— —— AND MOSES, E. R., JR., " Palatograms Change with Rates of Articulation," *ibid.*, 16 (1940), 52–61.

STEVENS, S. S., AND DAVIS, H., *Hearing, Its Psychology and Physiology*. New York, 1938.

—— —— " Psychophysiological Acoustics: Pitch and Loudness," *Journ. Acoust. Soc. Am.*, 8 (1936), 1–13.

STIRLING, W. F., *The Pronunciation of Spanish*. Cambridge, 1935.

STOUT, B., " The Harmonic Structure of Vowels in Relation to Pitch and Intensity," *Journ. Acoust. Soc. Am.*, 10 (1938), 137–46.

Studies in Experimental Phonetics, Edited by G. W Gray. *Louisiana State University Studies*, Vol. 27. Baton Rouge, 1936.

SÜTTERLIN, L., *Die Lehre von der Lautbildung*. Leipzig, 1908.

SWADESH, M., " A Method for Phonetic Accuracy and Speed," *Am. Anthropol.*, 39 (1937), 728–32.

SWADESH, M., " The Phonemic Interpretation of Long Consonants," *Lang.*, 13 (1937), 1–10.

—— " The Phonemic Principle," *ibid.*, 10 (1934), 117–29.

—— " The Phonetics of Chitimacha," *ibid.*, 10 (1934), 345–62.

—— AND VOEGELIN, C. F., " A Problem in Phonological Alternation," *ibid.*, 15 (1939), 1–10.

SWEET, H., *Collected Papers of Henry Sweet*, Arranged by H. C. Wyld. Oxford, 1913.

—— *A Primer of Phonetics*, Third Edition. Oxford, 1906.

—— *The Sounds of English*, Second Edition. Oxford, 1910.

TIFFIN, J., " The Psychophysics of the Vibrato," *Psychological Monographs*, 41, No. 4 (1931), 153–200.

Transactions of the American Academy of Ophthalmology and Otolaryngology, 41 (1936), 631–34.

Transactions of the American Laryngological Association, 55 (1933), 29–42.

TRAVIS, L. E., *Speech Pathology*. New York, 1931.

TROFIMOV, M. V., AND JONES, D., *The Pronunciation of Russian*. Cambridge, 1923.

TRUBETZKOY, N. S., *Anleitung zu phonologischen Beschreibungen*. Édition du Cercle linguistique de Prague. Brno, 1935.

TWADDELL, W. F., *On Defining the Phoneme, Language Monographs*, Vol. 16. Baltimore, 1935.

VACHEK, J., " Several Thoughts on Several Statements of the Phoneme Theory," *Am. Speech*, 10 (1935), 243–55.

Vibrato, The, Edited by C. E. Seashore. *Univ. Iowa Studies, Studies in the Psychology of Music*, Vol. I. Iowa City, 1932.

VIËTOR, W., *Elemente der Phonetik*, Seventh Edition. Leipzig, 1923.

—— *German Pronunciation, Practice and Theory*, Fifth Edition. Leipzig, 1913.

VOEGELIN, C. F., " Shawnee Phonemes," *Lang.*, 11 (1935), 23–37.

—— *Shawnee Stems and the Jacob P. Dunn Miami Dictionary*, Parts 1–4, in *Prehistory Research Series*, Vol. I. Parts 3, 5, 8, 9. Indianapolis, 1938–40.

VON HORNBOSTEL, E. M., " African Negro Music," *Africa*, 1 (1928), 30–62.

VON MEYER, G. H., *The Organs of Speech, and Their Application in the Formation of Articulate Sounds. International Scientific Series*, Vol. 46. New York, 1884.

WARD, I. C., *An Introduction to the Ibo Language*. Cambridge, 1936.

—— " Phonetic Phenomena in African Languages," *Archiv für vergleichende Phonetik*, 1 (1937), 51–52.

WARD, I. C., *Practical Suggestions for the Learning of an African Language in the Field*. Memorandum 14, International Institute of African Languages and Cultures. London, 1937.

Webster's New International Dictionary of the English Language, W. A. Neilson, Editor in Chief, Second Edition. Springfield, 1935.

WESTERMANN, D., AND WARD, I. C., *Practical Phonetics for Students of African Languages*. London, 1933.

YOUNG, E. H., *Overcoming Cleft Palate Speech, Help for Parents and Trainers*. Minneapolis, 1928.

ZWAARDEMAKER, H., " L'Analogue graphique de l'écriture analphabétique par signes de Jespersen en phonétique," *Arch. Néer. Phon. Expér.*, 1 (1927), 49–85.

INDEX